Praise for *Become Your Own Boss in 12 Months*

"*Become Your Own Boss in 12 Months* is a great handbook that can guide you through every step as you start and grow your small business."

—**Steve Mariotti**
Founder, National Foundation for
Teaching Entrepreneurship (NFTE)

"Don't even think about going into business without reading this book. The antidote to our current impulse-driven, needed-it-yesterday, get-rich-overnight epidemic, Melinda's book provides practical entrepreneurial Rx for anyone who has ever dreamed of working for themselves. A must for every entrepreneur's business reference shelf."

—**Christina Katz**
Author, *Get Known Before the Book Deal* and *Writer Mama*

"Melinda Emerson has written a remarkable book. It is essential reading for anyone seeking to make the transition from working girl to successfully working it, as an entrepreneur."

—**Cynthia McClain-Hill**
Past President, National Association
of Women Business Owners

"The perfect companion for those planning to go out on their own. Melinda delivers firsthand practical advice on how to be the successful entrepreneur. Read it if you want to get it right the first time."

—Kenneth L. Shropshire
David W. Hauck, Professor at the Wharton
School of Business, University of Pennsylvania

"Now there are no more excuses. Melinda's step-by-step approach has made it plain and simple. The only missing ingredient is you."

—Mel Gravely, PhD
Author, *Making It Your Business:
The Personal Transition from Employee to Entrepreneur*

"Melinda Emerson's *Become Your Own Boss in 12 Months* touches every topic a successful entrepreneur needs to know. This is a book that I will recommend to many who seek my advice about the life and choices of a budding entrepreneur."

—Lucy Rueben, PhD
Professor, Fuqua School of Business, Duke University

"Melinda Emerson is one of America's pioneering and passionate entrepreneurs. Her efforts to share her experiences will no doubt inspire others to pursue their own entrepreneurial vision with the same determination and vigor that has made her successful."

—Marc H. Morial
President, National Urban League

"Great step-by-step advice for anyone looking to start their own business."

—Andrew C. Taylor
Chairman and CEO, Enterprise Rent-A-Car

"What makes this book powerful, however, is that it goes beyond how to start a business—it is about integrating personal and professional passions—and practical ways to achieve that. This is one of those books you will read and re-read—and give extra copies to special friends."

—Sharon Hadary
Former Executive Director, Center for Women's Business Research

"Melinda Emerson knows what works in real life. That's why she gives you a detailed timeline to follow. She describes her twelve-month planning system as 'your personal GPS' and indeed it can keep you from getting lost."

—Paul B. Brown
Coauthor of the international bestseller *Customers for Life*

"Melinda made me do this, see this, and think this according to these steps for my business—so I know this is real stuff that folks need to hear and know that it works!"

—Anisha Robinson
Small Business Owner
LanceLee Planning

"In *Become Your Own Boss in 12 Months*, Melinda provides a witty and entertaining 'how-to' guide for entrepreneurs. It provides a step-by-step plan for developing a business model and building a dream. The book is a must-have for anyone who is considering starting a new business."

—Kathryn Y. Dove, Esquire
Professor of Business Law
National American University

"*Become Your Own Boss in 12 Months* offers a complete starters package for the budding entrepreneur and serves as a professional development course for seasoned entrepreneurs with plans of business expansion."

—Will Gist
Gist Enterprises

BECOME YOUR OWN BOSS IN 12 MONTHS

A Month-by-Month Guide to a Business That *Works*

MELINDA F. EMERSON

Foreword by Michael J. Critelli, Former CEO, Pitney Bowes

A
BUSINESS

Avon, Massachusetts

For my JoJo. Mommy loves you.

Copyright © 2010 by Melinda F. Emerson
All rights reserved. This book, or parts thereof, may not be reproduced
in any form without permission from the publisher; exceptions are
made for brief excerpts used in published reviews.

Published by Adams Business, an imprint of Adams Media,
a division of F+W Media, Inc.
57 Littlefield Street, Avon, MA 02322. U.S.A.
www.adamsmedia.com

ISBN 10: 1-60550-111-5
ISBN 13: 978-1-60550-111-6

Printed in the United States of America.

10 9 8 7 6 5 4 3

Library of Congress Cataloging-in-Publication Data
is available from the publisher.

This book is available at quantity discounts for bulk purchases.
For information, call 1-800-289-0963.

CONTENTS

PART I—GET READY!   17

PART II—GET SET!   71

Acknowledgments

I must honor my parents—my father, the late John E. Emerson, and my mother, Carrie Blocker Emerson. When I was a child, they always told me I could do anything. Again and again they scraped together money so that I could be exposed to the best the world had to offer.

Let me also thank my husband, Joseph Heastie. You helped me to write my first business plan line by line and gave me $500 to open my first business bank account. I thank you for your sacrifice for my entrepreneurial dream. I feel blessed to have my in-laws, Joe and Ernestine Heastie in my life. Big thanks to my three brothers, Eric for helpful legal advice and Rodney, who thought this would make a great book way back when it was just an idea. Patrick—your big sis loves you dearly. It is a blessing to come from a wonderful family. The Emerson, Blocker, Heastie, Taliaferro, Draper, Bailey, Copeland, and Seaton families are bedrocks of love and support. Special thanks to Aunt Lillian and Uncle Ricky, Aunt Betty and Uncle Curt, and my favorite cousin, Derik Blocker. You will never know how much your love and support has always meant to me.

Special thanks to Gerda Gallop-Goodman, Robyn Roberts, Gina Stikes, Meta Mereday, Lorna Neysmith, and Janet Hill-Talbert. They looked at this book at various stages line by line and made sure it was on point. I must thank Morris Anderson, Mike Pearson, Big Al Bullock, Dr. Hayward Farrar, Eliu Cornielle, Jin Hong Kim, Michael Leftwich, Vince Wright, Bill Dorsey, Glenn Brooks, Excell Lafayette, and Jim Mattera. More people need to be like you guys.

To my big sisters and mentors, I thank you for your kindness and patience. They are Cynthia Vivian, Avis Yates, Cindy Wollman, Cynthia McClain-Hill, Leslie Esdaile Banks, Elva Bankins, Sharon Rossmark, Terri Dean, Joanne Harmelin, Roz McPherson, Joanne Williams, Carole Copeland Thomas, Karyn Greenstreet, and Terry Goldston. For your love and friendship, thank you Kathryn Dove, Paulette Crawford, Ursula Doyle, Marilyn Thompson, Maria Morales, Lenette DeLoatch, Vikki Lassiter, Nicole Black, Shelby Banks, Kelly Lee, Renée Sloan, Cassandra Hayes, Pat Brown, Phillipa Ashby, Jennifer Braxton, Tina Evans Caines, Vernice Black Lewis, Evangelia Biddy, Nicole Whittington, Yvonne Yancy, Anisha Robinson, Tai Goodwin, Nicole Elie, and Eleanor Barber. You gals are irreplaceable. To my assistant Sonia Schenker, my publicists Don Lafferty and LiRon Anderson-Bell, and my marketing team Cathy Larkin and Scott Bradley, I thank you.

I have an incredible kitchen cabinet who helped me strategize about this book. Thank you Paul B. Brown, Laron Barber, Kevin Boston, Cathy Larkin, John Reddish, Taris Mullins, Ray McKee, Mark Corbin, Gerry Davis, Mary Meder, Paula Miller-Lester, Charles Dupree, George Miles, Sharon G. Hadary, Gwen Martin, Cheryl Beth Kuckler, Sally Solis-Cohen, E. Steven Collins, Lisa Duhart Collins, Harold Strong, Will Gist, Maurice Goodman, and Mel Gravely.

My editor Peter Archer and the Adams Media family have been fantastic to work with for this project. Thanks to everyone in production, design, marketing, publicity and sales. Peter, you are the best coach a first-time author could ever have. Thank you for your kindness and constant support.

The Urban League has meant so much to me. Special thanks to NUL CEO Marc Morial and my former chairman Michael Critelli of Pitney Bowes and the rest of my Urban League family. Thank you Robert D. Taylor, Paul McKinnon, Eric Eve, Rod Gilliam, Jim Winestock, Cathy Hughes, Hugh Price, Alexis Herman, Bill Mays, Cal

Darden, Effenus Henderson, Rodney Slater, Andy Taylor, Alonzo Byrd, Christie Conrad, Robert W. Sorrell, Wanda Paul, Michael Rashid, Pat Coulter, and Bruce Crawley. Thank you for your mentorship and friendship. I must thank my State Farm agent Edmund Nelson and his wife Cynthia and their staff. I also must thank my lawyers Sherman Smith and Tonya Evans-Walls and my bankers Carol Lawrence, Lisa Mann, and Kelly Finch. I was inspired to get serious about finishing this book after I attended a National Speaker Association workshop led by C. Leslie Charles. NSA rocks!

Thanks so much to my stylist/makeup guru Tracey Evelyn Reed and my hair stylist, Loreen Brown.

FOREWORD

If this were just another book on how to start a business, I would not be sufficiently excited to write this foreword, even though I have known Melinda Emerson as a colleague on the National Urban League Board of Trustees for a number of years. This is one of the most insightful books I have read on any subject.

This book can be read and enjoyed on many levels. It is certainly a very high-quality guidebook on how to start a business. But what truly makes it stand out for me is the extent to which Melinda helps the reader to think through much deeper issues. She recognizes that starting a business is as much about defining the founder's core values and priorities as it is putting together a business plan to market the products and services. Although this book is uniformly excellent and each chapter could be the foundation for a separate, highly insightful book, some of the profound insights come from the many points Melinda helps the reader understand about how tightly interwoven the business owner's *life* goals are with *business* goals.

She makes it clear that the most critical success factor for a business owner is the ability of that owner to decide on life-related goals and to align the business to the achievement of those goals. She also reminds the reader that, like any goal of consequence, sacrifices are needed, and she is more explicit than other books about the kinds of sacrifices that will be required. Beyond that, she makes it clear that there are several different approaches to running a small business, each of which springs from a particular set of life priorities for the owner.

What also impresses me about the book is the extent to which it raises basic questions that enthusiastic business owners fail to address until it is too late. Most owners start businesses because they believe that a product or service that excites them and a group of investors will also excite customers. Even if they are right, she points out the less glamorous details about selling and marketing the product or service, how to support it after the customer acquires it, and how to ensure that the end-to-end value chain is profitable. I particularly liked her comments about the critical importance of customer support and service.

I also recall sharing a story with Melinda about a friend of mine who invested in a restaurant and came to the reluctant conclusion that its profitability depended more on decisions about napkins, water consumption, cash management, and electricity and health department compliance costs than the food, service, and décor that enamored the restaurant's critics. Throughout the book Melinda does a great job illustrating the importance of a wide range of seemingly mundane details that, if not attended to, can sink a business.

Although she is advising would-be small business owners, her advice applies equally to executives and professionals of large businesses. Having been on many sales calls at Pitney Bowes, I would underscore the importance of her comment, "You must capture your target's attention in the first *seven seconds* or you fail." As a recipient of sales solicitations, I have also found myself losing patience with numerous sales people long before the person told me what they were selling.

Another broader lesson for business people from organizations of all sizes is that we must not overlook opportunities that can arise at taxi stands, on an Amtrak train, and in churches and alumni associations. Whether one is representing a small or large business, we are all brand ambassadors for our businesses 24/7 and can make those encounters with others either moments of success or missed opportunities.

Finally, Melinda helps the prospective business owner think about the point in time when the founder will have to add employees or other helpers. To the degree that any of us wants an organization to outlast us and to leave a legacy of success, we will need to think about those who will take on the work we have started. You need to hire people only when the business has reached a stage at which adding staff makes sense and is supportable by the business' revenues. At the same time, you need to know when it is time to delegate work to someone else to free yourself up for higher value activity. The decision about when and how to add staff is challenging, and Melinda deals very effectively with both the conceptual and practical issues associated with hiring people.

In the course of preparing this foreword, I have read and re-read many parts of this book and found new insights each time. This is a book to be savored and to remain at close reach for a very long time, whether you are starting a business, running one, or simply interested in why some businesses succeed and others do not.

—**Michael Critelli**
Former CEO, Pitney Bowes
December 2009

How to Use This Book

What This Book Can Do for You

This book covers everything about starting your own business, from life planning and personal finance, to marketing and business plans, to financial management, launching your business, and handling customer complaints.

It is designed to help you set your personal long-term goals, clarify your personal and business financial picture, understand your personal strengths and weaknesses, develop timelines for your transition, focus your activities to achieve your transition, set business goals and measures, and anticipate as well as manage obstacles that you will likely come across in your business.

The Power of Planning

This twelve-month planning process is your personal GPS to starting a business and realizing your new life. We've all heard the saying, "You can never be too rich or too thin." In business, "you can never be too organized." Goals are dreams put to a timeline. Good ideas need a well-executed business strategy and backup plans. Before you write a business plan, you must develop a *life plan*. This book will help aspiring entrepreneurs understand and draft a solid personal plan and from that derive a strong business plan.

Plan Your Transition

People do not leave a job, they leave people. If you're sick of your boss and want to work for yourself, you may be tempted to hand in your resignation tomorrow.

Instead of quitting a job in haste, which will significantly impact your household, slow down! Count to ten and start *planning* your escape from corporate America. Take the time to get your personal house in order so that you can quit your job with a blueprint that will minimize the financial hardship for yourself and your family. As an aspiring entrepreneur, this book will help you financially reposition yourself.

Framework of Fortitude

Do you have the courage, persistence, confidence, skills, work ethic, and focus needed to succeed as an entrepreneur? On top of that, do you have the ability to do all the jobs entrepreneurs must do? As your own boss, you'll be chief salesperson, secretary, payroll clerk, IT technician, and HR manager. Once you make a sale, then you must service the customer, too. This book explains the skills you must have or learn to make your dream a business reality.

Turn Your Notion into Knowledge

Most people dream about owning and running a business. You may have had a "notion" for years that someday you would be president of a company, successful beyond your wildest dreams. Turning that dream into reality is an evolutionary process. It involves not only having a solid business idea but also knowing the "business of running a business." You will need to get your arms around stuff like accounting principles, legal issues, operation requirements, banking relationships and processes, and the needed human, branding, and financial management skills. This book will reduce your learning curve about starting and running your small business.

Identify Your Niche Market

Too many small business owners make the mistake of trying to sell from too big a basket of goods and services. Make sure your basket is just big enough so that you can cater to your customers' needs while realizing a profit.

Sometimes you'll have to turn down business if it doesn't fit in with your core business. Given limited time and resources, a niche focus is the best and most efficient strategy for a small business. Focusing on a specific customer/industry allows you to make the most of your marketing dollars. This book will help you develop a targeted marketing plan that will increase your probability of success.

Focus on Finance

If you are not thinking about your enterprise making money everyday, then you have an expensive hobby. Too many small businesses operate at a net loss and do not realize this until it's too late. A large number of small firms fail because they do not operate professionally or employ strict fiscal discipline. There are many money-draining traps that can snare small business owners. Like it or not, the money you make is your report card and there is no room for an "F." This book will tell you about pricing strategy and managing cash flow in and out of your business.

Solutions for Success

Business success is rarely a straight line to the top. It is not enough to have a plan "A"; you must be flexible. You need a plan "B" and even a plan "C" to sidestep obstacles in your business. Problems are inevitable. Anything can happen—from needing alternative suppliers, changing your product mix, or adjusting your prices to new competition or reinventing your value proposition. "Solution" thinking is the only remedy. When you are a start-up business, two things can quickly take down your business: lack of planning and lack of experience. This book will make you aware of the common mistakes that can snare a start-up entrepreneur.

The timeline I lay out in this book is ideal; it is not meant to be restrictive. If you have strong financial reserves you might fly through this book and start your business in six months. Or it could take you eighteen months to follow the steps. It doesn't matter, as long as you have a plan.

To achieve success as a small business owner, you need to be flexible, pay close attention to your market, and figure out what you do *not* know about running a business. To start, you need two plans— one for yourself and one for your new enterprise.

1

So You Think You Want to Be an Entrepreneur

Before I became a parent, people told me that the first five years are the toughest years for parents. That little person is dependent on you from the moment of conception to the day you put him or her on the yellow cheese wagon headed for kindergarten. Your job isn't over once your child is going to school full-time, but at that point children can do some things for themselves.

The same is true for a small business. If you think that you work hard now, just wait until you become your own boss. You will come to know what the word "sacrifice" means. You'll scale back eating out, buying the latest gadget, and shopping whenever you feel like it. You'll cook at home and eliminate all unnecessary spending. Yes, that well-deserved steak dinner at your favorite restaurant is now an unnecessary expense. Small businesses typically take twelve to eighteen months to break even and three years to generate any profits. And it usually takes four years of focused effort for a business to blossom into a self-sustaining entity. It will take every bit of enthusiasm and energy you have to grow your business into a viable enterprise and a powerful brand.

Being a successful entrepreneur is also about having patience. You need to be patient with yourself, your employees, and most importantly, your customers. The sales won't come as fast as you think they should, but if you can just hold on, being an entrepreneur can be your most satisfying professional experience.

So the first step is to decide if you're cut out to live this kind of life.

The Entrepreneurial Mindset

- You always think there's a better way to do things.
- You'd prefer to be in charge.
- You think your boss is generally clueless.
- You feel underused by your supervisors and dissatisfied by your job.
- You know you would do things differently if it were your company.
- You sit at your desk calculating the amount of money you make for your employer, thinking that you should be working for yourself.
- You are convinced that you could do a better job than the folks that surround you.

Entrepreneurs are natural leaders. They are self-motivated and creative thinkers. They can make a decision quickly and stick to it. Entrepreneurs are visionaries, hard workers, and are extremely perceptive. They typically have demanding personalities and are extroverted. They are risk takers who are always seeking to improve upon current conditions.

On the flip side, at times such people are often stubborn and impatient. Entrepreneurs are not always good listeners or coachable, and can be territorial.

If any of this strikes a chord, if you feel these are qualities you possess, then entrepreneurship may be for you. But before you go into business, there are six things you must have:

1. A life plan
2. A solid business idea
3. Good credit and strong finances
4. A business plan
5. A supportive family or spouse
6. Faith

The Life of a Small Business Person

Becoming your own boss means more than sacrifice. It means long, hard, consistent work, often with the rewards still far off in the future. That's why you need a life plan before you decide to start your own business. You need to evaluate what you want out of life.

Consider the following questions:

- What kind of lifestyle do you want to have as an entrepreneur?
- How big do you want your business to get in terms of profits and staff?
- Will you have employees?
- How many hours a week will you work?
- Do you need to meet the school bus every day or take off every Friday?

- Are you willing to work seven days a week? For how many years can you keep that up?
- Will you need a partner? Could you handle working with one?
- How will you fund your household while you start your business?

You may have a great business idea, but you must decide if it's a good business for you and your family. Try this exercise: Close your eyes and think hard about what the best day in your business will look like five years from now. It may help if you write it down. Spend some time on it and get it fixed in your head.

Once you have that vision, consider what it will mean to you and to those you love for that day to become a reality.

Your Business Idea

Even if you come to the conclusion that you can be an entrepreneur, you must decide if you should. In other words, do you have a solid business idea? On a blank piece of paper, write down answers to the following questions:

- What problem are you solving for your customer?
- Does your business solve some unmet need?
- How much competition is there in your market?
- How will your business be different?
- Will you sell wholesale, retail, or both?
- Will you need a foreign manufacturing partner?

Researching the industry and the potential customer is crucial. Your research will also help determine whether there's a viable market for your product or service.

Know your business

Your business venture should be something in which you have experience or professional training. The only exception to this rule is if you buy into a franchise or take over an existing business. In those cases, the franchise company typically provides some training or there are people working in the business who can help provide institutional information about the business. (Even in those cases, I would not suggest buying a food franchise if you have never worked in a restaurant.) I hold a degree in communications studies from Virginia Tech and I worked six years in television as a news producer before I started my multimedia production company. Work for a business like the one you want to start for at least a couple of years before starting on your own. Do not start a daycare center if you have never worked with kids, just because you heard those kinds of businesses make a lot of money.

Love the work

On those hard days when there's no money and plenty of work to do, your love for what you do will be the only thing that keeps you going. Also, when you love what you do, your customers can see that, and they will be that much more interested in doing business with you. Savvy business owners figure out how to do something they are passionate about and get paid for it.

Consider business education

If you're in college and you think that you might ever want to start a business, double major or at least minor in business. It pays to know marketing strategy, finance, and accounting basics when you start a business. If you are still in school and are already interested in starting your own business, write an outline of your business ideas now.

As a business owner, you must constantly look for ways to improve yourself. Since I have been in business, I have been on the lookout for workshops, classes, or seminars on leadership and business. Whatever stage your business is in, you can always improve how you do things and learn something that can help your business grow. Start a library of books about small business, marketing, finance, sales, and leadership. At the end of this book, in the resource guide section, I have provided a list of the top ten small business books that every entrepreneur should read. Use this list to gather even more information about running a business.

EMERSON'S experience

There is always something that inspires or drives someone to become an entrepreneur. In my case, my personality did not quite jibe with the politics of the television newsroom in which I worked. After three television news jobs, I decided I had to figure out another way to earn a living. Seven years earlier, as a sophomore in college, I had been inspired by Oprah Winfrey, who started Harpo Productions. I decided that one day I would have my own production company.

When I started my business, I had no idea how to use basic spreadsheet or presentation software. I barely knew Microsoft Word. One of my mentors let me call her administrative assistant and ask questions about how to format business letters, mail merges, and such. At times, I would e-mail her a document, and she would format it for me. I am sure I gave her headaches, but she graciously gave me the support I needed. I invested in computer-based training to learn the software I would be using. To this day, I always remember this generous woman with a Christmas gift.

How are your people skills?

Your ability to interact with people, including customers, staff, and strategic partners, will be critical to your business success. Many entrepreneurs get frustrated with managing employees, even if they have experience managing people in a corporate setting. If you are a business owner who has never dealt with external customers or worked in a team environment, your people skills may need some work.

It all comes down to communication. Consider what you're trying to accomplish and do your best to determine what level of communication is required. It could be a face-to-face discussion, a memo, an e-mail, a handwritten note, or a phone call. Or you may need to use more than one method. Try to always end any interaction by recapping deliverables and any action items. Do not hesitate to follow up any communication in writing.

It's about the Money

Of course, the best business idea in the world isn't worth anything if you run out of money. There's no way around it: starting a business is expensive. It will be a while before you see a return on your investment. That's why, before you hand the boss your walking papers and box up the personal things in your cubicle, you'd better make sure you and your family are on solid financial ground.

You'll need good credit, a strong relationship with your bank—since you'll be relying on them for loans in the future—and enough money to support your family for at least a year. Sometimes this can come in the form of your spouse's job, and sometimes it's the nest egg that you've saved and scrimped and scraped together. But whatever the case, it's essential that you start your business from a position of financial security. Otherwise, you're finished before you've started.

Follow the Business Plan for Success

Once you complete your life plan, an evaluation of your business idea, and your financial inventory, you will know what you want out of life as an entrepreneur and whether you've got the resources to get it. After your personal path is clear, it's time to formulate your business model. Draw on the research you've already done on your industry; learn the trends and make sure you understand how big the potential market is for your product or service.

EMERSON'S essentials

Every small business needs a plan. You cannot be in business successfully without a business plan. *Just as you would never take a trip without knowing how much money you were going to need for the whole vacation, how long it was going to take you to get to your destination, and where you were going to stop overnight, you can't start a business without knowing its costs and structure.*

Everyone has great ideas, but ideas do not become businesses until they are written down as a plan. Writing a business plan is not as hard as you may think. Go to an office-supply store or purchase business plan software online to help you get started. Pace yourself. Write or research for just two hours a day, before work, or after the kids go to bed. Plan to invest enough time to get it right; my first business plan took me more than two months to complete.

After making a dent in your business plan with the software, take a business plan course from a nonprofit business training organization, a Small Business Development Center (SBDC), a Women's Business Development Center (WBDC), or a community college in your area. Remember: *Until you have a complete business plan with financial projections, you are a person with an idea. You are not in business!* Tim Berry, noted business planning expert, says not having a business plan is like walking down a major city street with a blindfold on. Do not put your business at a disadvantage, by not setting measurable goals for yourself and developing a budget for your business. You'll need a business plan to present to investors or bankers to get a small business loan. No one will loan you money for your idea without a business plan that has realistic financial projections.

EMERSON'S experience

I have rewritten my business plan every year that I have been in business. The third time I rewrote my business plan, I won a business plan competition in Philadelphia. The prize was $20,000 and free office space for a year.

Plans change once exposed to the market. In the first year or two of your business, you must revisit your business plan every two to three months to see what has changed and update it to reflect the market conditions. This is your blueprint to stay on top of your business goals and projections.

A Supportive Family or Spouse

Business owners who are married can benefit from a spouse who supports the household financially and provides health benefits while the enterprise is getting off the ground. However, suddenly becoming a one-salary family is tricky. Make sure that your spouse is behind your decision. If not, your dream can turn into a nightmare. It is very hard to start a business. If you come home to negativity every night, your likelihood of success is that much tougher.

Treat your spouse, who is sacrificing alongside you, like your number-one customer. Make sure there's good communication between you. Show appreciation for the partner who works the 9 to 5 and takes care of homework, dinner, and bed and baths for the kids most of the time. Remember that eventually your spouse will want to see money coming in the door instead of going out.

Gotta Have Faith

If your business is a recipe, I believe faith is a key ingredient. Faith gives you the confidence to quit your job and the courage to go forward. You will need faith the most on those days when things do not work out. Faith in your business will help you make it right with the client, learn from your mistakes, lick your wounds, and fight another day. Faith will help you trust your employees, vendors, and your customers. Religious or not, you can always pray.

Is Entrepreneurship for You?

If, after reading the section above, you put down this book and put your dream of entrepreneurship on the shelf, don't feel bad. Not everyone is cut out to be an entrepreneur. But if you've read to this point and your passion and commitment and faith are still strong . . . go for it!

2

WHY DOES IT TAKE TWELVE MONTHS?

Karen had a small business knitting custom scarves at her kitchen table. One day, a man at her doctor's office asked her about the lovely knit scarf she was wearing. She explained that she made it. The man's wife was a department store buyer, and he was looking for a unique gift for her birthday.

Karen knitted a special scarf for his wife. The woman liked it so much she wanted to stock it in her store to test the market. If it did well, she planned to put the item in stores across the country.

The buyer asked Karen for 200 scarves. Without thinking, Karen said, "Sure. I'll have them in sixty days." But she had no manufacturer. She made all her scarves by hand.

Two friends from her knitting class helped her to produce the first order, but she knew she could not keep up with the demand. Karen worked night and day to deliver her product. At the same time, she feverishly cruised the Internet looking for suppliers and manufacturers. She quickly realized that her price point was too low to use an American manufacturer, so she started looking abroad.

After signing with an overseas manufacturer, she thought she'd solved the problem. But because of her inexperience, she didn't factor in the time it takes overseas items to clear customs. Due to the delay, she missed her shipment to the department store. The store canceled her order. In the end, she lost a great deal of money on the transaction.

Author Stephen R. Covey says, "Begin with the end in mind." That is true in life and in business. When you design your business, you must decide how much you can take on and how big you want your operation to become, and plan accordingly.

Why Does It Take Twelve Months to Plan?

What's special about a twelve-month timeline for starting a small business? After coaching multitudes of entrepreneurs, talking with small business experts across the country, and as I considered all of the expensive mistakes that I made early on in my first business, I developed the Emerson Planning System, a twelve-month process to transition from a job to small business ownership.

To see why it takes a year, ask yourself if you have:

- A 700 or higher credit score
- Zero debt (including no car payments)

Then consider if you have the following cash reserves:

- Six month's salary in emergency savings
- Twelve months of monthly budget to run your household
- The first year of operating expenses to start the business

These are the financial requirements for starting a business! Repositioning yourself financially may take a year or more. There's no shortcut. When you first start out in business, your personal credit is your business credit. Banks typically do not extend loans or lines of credit until you've been in business two to three years. There are a few franchises that you can buy into that provide lending support, but it is still rare for a start-up to be able to borrow money. In the beginning, your credit cards, home equity, 401K, savings, and loans from family and friends are all you will have to start. Then, hopefully, your next funding will come from your customers.

And this doesn't take into account the time needed to develop your life plan, validate your business idea, develop your marketing strategy, your business plan, and to get in place all the elements of your day-to-day operations. As you move through this book, you'll see why I've attached a twelve-month timeline to the process.

Consider these statistics:

- It takes twelve to eighteen months to break even and typically three years for a small business to earn a profit.
- Less than 4 percent of all small businesses in the United States ever gross over $1 million in revenue.
- One in three small business owners will go out of business within the second year of operation.
- Eighty-two percent will go out of business by their fifth year in business.

For these reasons, I encourage you to think carefully about timing your decision to quit your job. You're doing yourself no favors by leaving your job prematurely. My twelve-month planning system is a plan for long-term success.

Additional Resource

Over the years, I have become so concerned about the general naiveté of would-be entrepreneurs that I wrote a special report on the subject, *44 Things To Do Before Going Into Business*, which is available as a free download on my website, *www.melinda emerson.com*. This report became the basis for the book that you are reading.

EMERSON'S essentials

You need to develop a life plan before you ever write a business plan. *Too many entrepreneurs underestimate and romanticize what is required to run a small business. Because starting your own business will mean such a radical shift in your lifestyle, you need to think through what this will mean. Only then are you ready to get into the nitty-gritty of your business planning.*

What if you don't have twelve months?

A year to plan and launch your business is ideal. Have people done it more quickly? Sure. Sometimes people are forced to start sooner. They're laid off, get fired, or receive great early retirement packages. Needing an immediate source of revenue, they put their enterprises on the fast track.

I only planned for three months with my first business. The downside—and it's a big one—is I learned plenty of expensive lessons. If you live by a budget, have your debt under control, and a significant amount of savings, you may well be able to start your business sooner than twelve months. Others may take more than a year to get personal finances in order. But the point is that with such a tight economy, no entrepreneur can afford to waste time, resources, or any opportunities making expensive mistakes. Once you start, you will get some on-the-job training, but that's a luxury, and you can't afford to waste it on things you should have known before you opened your doors. The Emerson Planning System gives you time to evaluate your life, gain control over your finances first, validate your business concept, and then start a business.

Hard times bring great innovations

Do not get discouraged in tight economic times. Great inventions and businesses have developed during difficult financial times in U.S. history. Take a look at the inventions below. The stock market crash of 1929 knocked the U.S. economy back nearly ten years and created the Great Depression. At that time, people had to become as entrepreneurial as possible.

Here are some Depression-era inventions:

- **1929**—Clarence Birdseye offers his quick-frozen foods to the public.
- **1930**—Richard D. Drew invented a clear cellulose tape called Scotch Brand Cellulose Tape.
- **1930**—Ruth Wakefield invented chocolate chips (and chocolate chip cookies). Wakefield ran the Toll House Inn in Whitman, Massachusetts. Her new invention was called the "Toll House Cookie."

Think of this book as a reference guide. It walks you through each phase of planning—from your first brilliant idea, through life planning, financial repositioning, evaluating your business concept, developing a marketing plan, and writing your business plan, all the way up to your first day of business. It takes more than a notion to get started down the path of entrepreneurship. It all starts with a timely idea, then requires hiring the right professionals to put a proper business structure around it. By following the Emerson Planning System, you will shorten your learning curve to starting your small business.

When you start a business, your time and money are on the line, and so are your dreams. Don't put them at risk by not doing enough research and thoughtful planning.

There are six stages in the Emerson Planning System. This book walks you through the month-by-month planning system and through your first year in business. See the diagram below.

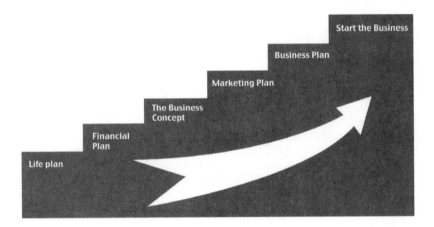

This is a great time to explore your entrepreneurial side; you just need to make sure that the business you start is the right business for you. This planning process may seem like an exercise, but it's really an opportunity to think everything through. You will be able to personally plan, grow, and research your business idea to make sure you are ready to meet the task of starting your small business.

PART I

GET READY!

Sunday	Monday	Tuesday	Wednesday	Thursday	Friday	Saturday
				1	2	3
4	5	6	7	8	9	10
11	12	13	14	15	16	17
18	19	20	21	22	23	24
25	26	27	28	29	30	31

3

GET YOUR LIFE PLAN
TOGETHER

⎡ *Your twelve-month countdown clock* ⎤
  starts with this chapter

What is a life plan? It's a way to identify your motivation, skills, and personal goals. Essentially, it's how you figure out what you really want out of life. When you start a business you must align your personal and professional lives. Developing a life plan is the best way to achieve that. Before your business opens its doors, there are ten questions you must answer. You probably will not be able to answer all of them right away, but over the next twelve months, keep coming back to this list until you've got answers for all of them.

1. Why do I want to start a business?
2. Do I have the entrepreneurial mindset?
3. Do I have the energy to start this business?

4. How much money do I have saved to start this business and cover household emergencies?
5. Do I have a supportive spouse or family?
6. How long can my household operate without me generating an income?
7. What do I know about the industry and what do I need to learn?
8. Is there demand for my product or service?
9. How is my product different from the competition?
10. Do I have the confidence and skill to run a business?

EMERSON'S essentials

Everyone has tangible skills, but not everyone has all the skills needed to run a business. *Developing a life plan will help you determine what abilities you have and what skills you need to learn or to find in an employee or partner.*

Just the Facts

When you start to consider your life plan and what you want it to look like, you can't succumb to emotion. You need to stay focused on the facts and separate them from your feelings. I can't think of a better story to illustrate this point than the following:

Among my early coaching clients were the owners of a restaurant and a catering company. The husband was the chef, while his wife kept an eye on operations. Neither had a background in business. Their food was great and they had a good reputation, but their enterprise consistently operated in crisis mode.

I suggested they find a partner or investor, preferably someone with experience in the food industry. The wife was all for it, but the chef was a proud man. He agonized over relinquishing financial control to an investor. He delayed making a decision until he was nearly in financial ruin. Eventually he brought in an investor to save his business.

The chef couldn't separate his desire for control from the need for someone in the business with stronger entrepreneurial skills. As a result, he ruined his personal credit and almost wrecked his business.

EMERSON'S essentials

Business decisions must be made on the basis of factual financial data and not emotion. *The most successful entrepreneurs keep up-to-date financial records and let the facts drive business decisions.*

I know a woman who quit her corporate job to start a Rita's Water Ice franchise. She was very excited and couldn't wait to pick out her location, develop her marketing plan, and open her doors. She told everyone about her new business. Two years went by, and I bumped into her and asked how it was going. She said, "I sold my business. I realized that I cannot be a slave to anything, especially something that doesn't fulfill me. On top of that, I hated managing teenagers. It was a bad deal all the way around. I'm now grateful to be back in a corporate job."

The seven-days-a-week, open-to-close lifestyle was not right for this woman. If she had taken the time to think through a life plan before starting the business, she probably never would have bought the franchise. You must fully understand your motivations up front, so that you can figure out how best to set up your business and the level of commitment it will take. *Your business plan must align with your life plan. If it doesn't, the business will fail.*

People who have an entrepreneurial mindset are typically motivated by five basic things:

1. Control
2. Freedom
3. Money
4. Problem solving
5. Creativity

The trick is to determine which one motivates you the most. Ask yourself which of the following best describes your personality and your attitude toward work. Based on this information, you will be able to set up your company in a way that works best for you.

Control—You like control, power, and influence. You are highly self-motivated. You want to have control over the products and/or the operations. The question you must answer is: how much control do you require? Do you need it on a day-to-day basis, or is it enough to control the strategic direction of the company? You struggle to balance micromanagement with attention to detail.

Freedom—Flexibility is what you desire. You want to be in control of your life and how you work. You might be disillusioned with your job because you're not allowed to telecommute or work flextime hours. *You* need to determine where and when you work. Work/life balance is a major focus for you. You are driven by deadlines, but not necessarily structure.

Money—You have calculated how much money you make for your employer, and you believe you could and should be making the same amount for yourself. All entrepreneurs want and need to make money. How much money is the question? Are you looking to create a lifestyle business to provide a decent income and a couple of nice vacations a year, or do you want to buy your own island? Your answer will determine what kind of capital you will need and when. Whatever the case, you're clear that money is your main motivating factor.

Problem solving—You are a solution-oriented thinker. You want to help people. You like a challenge and are a risk-taker. This is good, since clients want solutions. On the downside, you have a tendency not to focus on finishing tasks. You have multiple projects going at one time. Over the long term, you sometimes struggle with a lack of focus.

Creativity—You are a big-idea person. You want your business and its products to be your legacy. You are all about innovation and process development. You believe there is a new and better way to do most things. At times, you neglect or resent feedback on your creative ideas, even if it might lead to improvement. At the same time, you're highly protective of your intellectual property so that someone else will not get the primary financial benefit from your great idea.

Rate yourself for each of these traits by giving it a number from 1 to 5, with 5 being Extremely Important and 1 being Not Important. This exercise will show your hierarchy of motivations.

ENTREPRENEURSHIP MOTIVATION SCALE

Control   _____

Freedom   _____

Money   _____

Problem-solving _____

Creativity   _____

Construct Your Life Plan

With the previous exercise, you've determined what motivates you. Now you need to see what that says about your plans to become an entrepreneur. I suggest you consider discussing this with your spouse or a group of close friends. Here are some further questions to get you started:

What is your passion? Is there an industry that fits your passion? Think about the types of things that you love to do, whether at work or at home. Do you have any hobbies that could be businesses? What would you do for free?

What do you know how to do? This is not a standard resume list. Instead, think back over all the jobs you've held. List all of your job duties and accomplishments in exhaustive detail. List your skills and accomplishments in your professional and personal life. Don't forget to include volunteer activities. Consider the skills you have that would be helpful in starting a business and managing it successfully.

In what way(s) are you a rock star? Are you a "killer" salesperson? Can you sell ice to an Eskimo? Are you an idea guy? Are you a great customer-relationship manager? Are you a number cruncher? Or, better yet, are you a technical wiz who's also a "killer" salesperson?

What do you do really, really well that you could sell? What have you been trained to do? Now, think about the other skills you have. Do you make furniture? Or make jewelry? Do home improvements? Or enjoy interior decorating?

What do you hate to do? Sometimes, what you do really well is something that you are trained to do, but it is not something you particularly like to do. If something makes your brain feel dead, you shouldn't make a career of doing it, even if you excel at this activity. In the long run, you'll burn yourself out and your business will fail.

Do you get bored easily? If so, rule out businesses that involve doing the very same thing for every customer. You will need a business that has a different challenge everyday.

What is your energy level? How long can you work at a stretch? For start-ups, fourteen- to sixteen-hour days are not uncommon. Consider your age and how family obligations will impact your energy level. Are you a parent with young children? Are you over fifty? Can you handle a start-up business and the administration of your household?

What are your technical skills? In today's fast-paced world, technology changes faster than the blink of an eye. Consider things such as your knowledge of customer relationship management software, PDAs, inventory management systems, e-commerce websites, merchant accounts, and accounting software. Can you see yourself entering your own data into QuickBooks? Are you a technophobe or eager to learn new things? Social media marketing is a great way to launch a new business, but the technology is changing constantly. Do you currently use LinkedIn, Twitter, Facebook, or YouTube? How about your website/blog development skills? Can you upload your own blog posts, edit your own podcasts, and record YouTube videos? If you can't operate the technology, the only alternative is hiring help. Can you afford technical help?

Now, do another exercise. This one you can do by yourself. Take thirty minutes and write down what your best day will look like five years from now.

EMERSON'S experience

BELOW IS AN EXCERPT FROM MY LIST OF SKILLS.

Supervised teams as large as twenty-five people, including graphic designers, writers, photographers, web developers, and animators.

Developed various marketing projects for broadcast or business use.

Developed and established company-wide policies and operating plans consistent with broad company objectives.

Directed and guided the planning and management of the company's production, research, and development activities.

Be bold! Consider things like ultimate vacations, hobbies, volunteer work, philanthropy, and early retirement goals. Leave out no detail. Know everything, down to what color the limousine is that picks you up and takes you to the *Oprah Winfrey Show*. You need to frequently remind yourself what your mission and purpose are, which is why it is critical to get clear about this from the very beginning.

Your Ideal Work

You have already considered your personal goals, motivations, the realities of your life, and the skills you have and need. It's time to figure out what kind of environment you like to work in.

- Do you need to be around people?
- Can you work from home, or do you need a structured office?
- Do you need flex hours to balance taking care of your family?
- How many days a week will you work in your business?

Below is a work style chart. Rate each of the issues according to its importance by giving it a number from 1 to 5, with 5 being Extremely Important and 1 being Not Important. You'll be able to see from this what kind of a setting you want to work in.

WORK STYLE SURVEY
I want to work a four-day work week _____
I am willing to work a six-day work week _____
I want to work from home _____
I want to work from an office _____
I want to work in an office setting with other people _____
I prefer to work behind the scenes _____
I like interacting with lots of people _____
I prefer limited travel _____
I don't mind lots of travel _____

Now you have an idea of where you want to go, what skills you already have and need, and what type of work style suits you best. This information will also let you see whether your business goals and your personal preferences are compatible. If you only want to work four days a week, running a retail store with extensive hours may not be for you.

Now comes the really important bit. Make a list of steps you'll need to take to achieve your life goals. Refer to this list often during the next twelve months. Your life plan will keep you focused so you can do what you love—and that always brings out the best in an entrepreneur.

EMERSON'S action steps

[1] Find visual images of your personal goals and make a life plan collage. Tape it on the wall in your work space or tack it up on the bulletin board in your home office.

[2] Keep your life plan in a visible place to constantly remind you of what you want, what's important, and what to do next.

[3] When making strategic decisions about your new business venture, begin by reviewing your life plan to ensure that your business goals remain in alignment with your life goals.

4

YOUR FINANCIAL PLAN

$$\Big[\ \textit{Eleven months before you start}\ \Big]$$

As you prepare to leap into entrepreneurship, you must focus on your finances. This will mean some long discussions with your family as you decide how to scale down your lifestyle to just your basic needs.

EMERSON'S experience

One of my classmates from Virginia Tech is a Shell Oil franchisee. When he first wanted to join the oil giant, he was told that the cost was $900,000 to lease one gas station. He figured he was a smart guy with a good business plan, driven by a franchising opportunity with a *Fortune* 100 company. He had an excellent business background and exceptional personal credit. He went to a few banks to borrow the money, and every single one turned him down. This often happens to start-up entrepreneurs. Banks typically are only interested in loaning money to businesses with a two- to three-year track record.

After being rejected by the third bank, he decided to come up with the money on his own. Fortunately, since his first job out of college he had saved 25-40 percent of every paycheck he ever made. He owned two houses, so he sold them both. He was an investor in an Internet business, and he sold his interest in that. He sold his car. He opened several new credit cards and took the cash advances on them. He was still short of the money he needed, so he went to his father for help. His parents took a second mortgage on their house. As a family, he and his parents came up with the $900,000 to acquire the first gas station. Five years later, they have twenty gas stations and are owners of a $100 million family business.

Your Personal Financial Goals

Ideally, you should achieve three personal financial goals prior to starting your business.

1. You should have zero debt
2. Your credit score should be 700 or higher
3. You should have twelve months' worth of household expenses in your savings account

Eliminate Personal Debt

Develop a plan to become debt free. Eliminating your debt will allow you to make decisions that are always in the best interest of your business and not due to pressure from creditors. Low or zero debt will enable you to free up your credit capacity. You will probably not be able to eliminate your mortgage or student loans, but everything else needs to go, especially credit cards. Pay off your car if you can. Get down to basic living expenses only, i.e., mortgage, phone, gas, electric, cable, food, etc. When I decided to leave my job to start my first business, I took out a home equity loan (if you decide to do this, you must apply while you are still working and can prove income) and paid off every bill I had, including my car loan. A home equity loan is advantageous because the interest can be written off against your income taxes.

Credit card management

Credit cards account for a huge portion of personal debt in this country. Make a list of all your credit card debt, the balance owed, and the interest rate for each card. Then choose the credit card with the lowest balance and work to pay that off. At the same time, continue to pay the minimum fees on the others cards to keep them current.

Once you've paid off one card, choose the card with the highest interest rate. Pick out one card to focus on at a time. Pay at least 10 percent more than the minimum each month, until you pay off the card.

Don't cut up your cards or cancel them. You will need those credit lines for your business. It doesn't matter how many credit cards you have, as long as you don't owe large amounts of money on them. More important is your borrowing power. You want to eliminate debt and protect your credit score at the same time.

Eliminate monthly payments

First, pay off obligations that will eliminate a monthly payment. For example, if you get a bonus of $5,000, use some of it to pay off the balance on your car. By doing so, you eliminate the $350 monthly payment from your household budget and increase your rate of savings.

Improve Your Credit Score

A good credit score is essential when starting out in business. You will be asking vendors and others to extend you credit. Before they do so, they will review your credit score—not your business, because that doesn't exist yet—your personal credit score. Your personal credit is your businesses' credit.

Before you sign a lease for retail space, the landlord will pull your credit score. If you need a merchant service account to accept credit cards, the vendor will pull your credit score. If you ever plan to borrow money or apply for a line of credit, your personal credit score is the most information in the application process.

Your score on the most commonly used index—the Fair Isaac Corporation or FICO—ranges from 560 to 800. For your business to avoid credit problems in its early stages, your personal score should be at least 700.

Managing Your Household Budget

You must run your household using a monthly budget; it's the best way the keep track of your expenses. Many people shy away from budgets because they think that they are about limiting spending. Think again! A budget is about planning your spending. Creating it should be a shared activity. For it to work, you and your spouse or partner should forge your budget together, understand its purpose, and agree upon its principles. Managing your household with a budget is a great skill to have because you will absolutely need to manage your business with a budget.

EMERSON'S essentials

TAKE THE TIME TO GET YOUR BUDGET RIGHT.

Use budget software to help track your spending (make sure to record all receipts).

Anticipate future expenses as much as possible.

Have an accountability partner, your spouse, a close friend or peer who can question you about a sudden shopping spree is who you want in this role.

To make a budget, take the following steps.

1. Write down your net income after taxes and deductions
2. List all of your major expense categories (mortgage, car payment, etc.)
3. Total all expenses
4. Subtract Total Expenses from Income
5. If a deficit appears, determine how to address it

You can earn additional income to cover a deficit; possibly one of you will need to get a second job for a while. You can make up the deficit out of your savings, but since your savings are limited, this is a losing game. Or you can reduce your expenses. If you're getting ready to start a business, the last option is probably the best.

Sample Budget for Family of Four

Monthly Expenses

Savings	$150
Mortgage	$2,000
Home equity loan	$200
Personal grooming	$150
Church donations	$100
Entertainment	$50
Dry cleaning	$40
Car note(s)	$300
Car maintenance, upkeep, and insurance	$225
Gas for two cars	$200
Food/household supplies	$300
Life insurance	$168
Prescriptions/co-pays	$45
Day care/aftercare	$760
Electric/gas	$180
Phone/cable/Internet	$150
Cell phone(s)	$300
Water	$47
Children activity costs	$80
Credit cards	$400
Total Household Costs	**$5,845**

Now you know what your monthly costs are. You also know that you must have twelve months of living expenses, or, in the above case, $70,140, in reserve before you open your business.

EMERSON'S essentials

If you can run your household with a monthly budget, you are far more likely to run your small business with a budget. *This will help you always stay on top of your company's expenses and profitability.*

Personal Cash Reserves

In fact, to be completely financially secure in your new venture, there are three pools of money you should have in a savings or money market account prior to starting your business:

- Six months of emergency savings for your household
- Twelve months of monthly budget to run your household
- The first year of operating expenses for your business

Make sure you understand all of your current and future household expenses as well as those your business will incur. It will help to track your family expenses for a month. Once you do that, you can start looking at ways to cut back. If you start modifying your spending habits a year before you quit your job, it won't seem so drastic when your paycheck is gone.

Determine how you will cover additional insurance costs. Since most people's health insurance is through their work, quitting your job will mean you're responsible for your own insurance. There are several types of policies you may need once you quit your job: health, disability, business liability, workman's compensation, and life insurance.

Options for health insurance

It's possible you may not need to buy this insurance entirely on your own. There are these options:

- Use your spouse's insurance through his/her job.
- Consider COBRA, a federal law that requires most employers with group health plans to offer former employees the opportunity to continue their health insurance for up to eighteen months.
- Secure an individual policy for the family and/or employees. Use a health broker to research your options, and don't worry about cost. Brokers are paid by the insurance companies, not by you. Trade associations and Chambers of Commerce are also good sources for individual policy options.

I highly recommend disability insurance, especially for single-income families. If you do physical work in dangerous environments or if your business will involve heavy lifting, i.e., you plan to work as a contractor, painter, security agent, florist, etc., disability insurance is a must.

EMERSON'S experience

When I was pregnant with my son, I had an extremely tough pregnancy. I was unable to work for nearly six months. I never could have imagined needing disability insurance, but I did. When you are an entrepreneur, if you do not work, you do not get paid.

Restructure Your Finances

As you move ahead with this part of your financial plan, take the following steps:

Get your credit report. Transunion, Equifax, and Experian Credit will each provide a free credit report once a year, but you must pay for your actual credit score. Get all three scores, as each credit bureau scores differently. You can also use *www.annualcreditreport.com* to get a free credit report.

Calculate your net worth. Net worth is your net assets minus your liabilities. Make sure to include cash values of the cars and any life insurance policies as net assets. Download a free form to help you calculate net worth from *www .melindaemerson.com.*

Pay your bills on time. Even if you don't have the full amount, send something and send it on time. Paying late fees is like throwing money away. Shift your bill paying online. Many banks offer free online banking. Some third party providers offer online services for a minimal cost. You can also arrange for many of your regular monthly bills to be automatically debited from your account.

Control Your Spending!

Some people make spending decisions based on what is in their pocket that day. Others treat their check card like free money. By living by a budget, you can take control of your spending. Use these simple rules to cut down excess spending and get a handle on other expenses.

Keep good records. Keep separate records for your business and personal finances. Religiously track all income and expenses, and save all of your receipts. Many expenses are tax deductible.

Before heading to the store, make a list of what you need and stick to it. Avoid impulse buying. Be careful not to go grocery shopping when you are hungry. A growling stomach makes it very hard to stick to your list.

Cut back on trips to Starbucks, Dunkin' Donuts, Dairy Queen, and Blockbuster. The money you spend each week on unnecessary extras can add up. Treat yourself once in a while, but don't make a habit of it. You'll be surprised how much money you'll save.

Avoid retail therapy. You can no longer afford to buy something shiny and new to make yourself feel better after a rough day at the office. Instead, develop a cost-free hobby. Start running or taking long, hot bubble baths.

Consider shutting off your home phone. Go cell phone only. Removing the landline can reduce your monthly expenses.

Review your insurance policies. Consider increasing your deductibles on your car and homeowners insurance. This will reduce your monthly or quarterly premiums.

Cook at home and bring your leftovers to work for lunch. Stop going to the corner lunch wagon. You'll save money, get a healthier meal, and spend more quality time with your family.

Park and ride. We are all feeling the effects of high gas prices. Consider using public transportation if it's available in your area. Talk to your coworkers who live in your area about carpooling.

Check out the library. You can borrow books, magazines, and the latest DVDs from the library and request that they order them for you. If you're a serious book junkie, find a good used bookstore or buy used books on Amazon.com.

Vacation at home. Hit the local news websites for what's going on around your town. Many cities sponsor free or low-cost events. You'll rediscover your hometown.

Drink at home. Stop drinking alcohol in bars and restaurants. Beer, wine, and mixed drinks are cheaper when you pour them yourself. Pick up a six-pack or a few bottles, invite over some friends you haven't seen in a while, and hang out at the house.

One of my mentors suggested, "You must ask yourself 'Why?' three times before you make any purchase." In other words, you should have three separate reasons before you can justify spending any of your precious (and limited) resources.

Start-up Funds Strategies

Launching your business is going to cost money, and it probably can't all come from savings. You need to evaluate where you will raise your start-up funds.

Determine how much equity you have in your home. Equity is the market value of your home, minus any mortgages or credit lines in use. You can often tap into that equity by getting a line of credit. Essentially, the home equity loan serves as a second mortgage. You can use this equity to finance your small business. The interest from a home equity line of credit can be written off on your income taxes.

Determine how much money you have coming to you from your company. Do you have unused vacation or sick time, a bonus, severance, or a buyout package? That's money you can cash out when you leave your current job.

Use the one-third rule. Whenever you get a bonus check, tax refund, or any occasional money, spend one-third on something you need or want, put one-third toward paying down debt, and put one-third toward your saving plan.

Your savings plan starts with your ability to control your spending and cut costs. You cannot kick an addiction to living from paycheck to paycheck all at once. It will be a gradual step-by-step process, but you can do it!

Before you implement these sweeping changes, have a family meeting to get buy-in from your partner or spouse and your children. Most importantly, *be* the change you want to see. Don't tell everyone else to stop spending and then buy something you do not need. Set an example and show that you are committed to your plan.

Your Banking Relationship

When your personal finances are in order, you need to begin setting up your banking arrangements for the business. Be careful not to look for money in the wrong places. One of the mistakes that small business owners make is not doing their homework before selecting a bank. If you use your personal bank as your business bank, you could lose everything if your business goes under, since the bank can seize your personal assets to satisfy your business debt. Do not use the same bank for your personal and business affairs.

EMERSON'S essentials

You are not just looking for a bank; you are looking for a banking relationship. *You want to find a bank that is interested in your business success and not just your deposits. Select a bank that is best for your business.*

Do not be swayed by television advertising when selecting a lending institution. The banks that are doing all the advertising may be the worst banks for your business. Remember that there's a big difference between the kind of services you'll need from your business bank and those you need from your personal bank.

Shop around. Ask your accountant. Ask fellow business owners about their experiences with their banks. Interview at least three branch managers at different banks before making your decision. The larger banks have a tendency to rotate small business bankers frequently, so it's important to know what is happening at the branch that you will be using. Ask the following questions:

- What percentage of your customers at this branch are small-business customers?
- How fast are checks cleared to my business account (in-state and out-of-state)?
- Is there a dedicated small-business banker on your staff? (If so, ask to meet him or her.)
- What kind of customer service do you provide for small businesses?
- Are loan decisions made locally?
- Does the small-business banker have any influence over the loan decision process?
- How many SBA loans did your bank process last year?

Once you decide on a bank, have lunch with your branch manger once or twice a year to discuss the status of your business and any exciting news (e.g., awards, major new clients/contracts, etc). Bankers love this, and it keeps them engaged in your success.

EMERSON'S action steps

[1] Build your credit score to 700 or higher.

[2] Develop a plan to eliminate all of your debt.

[3] Construct a household budget and stick to it.

[4] Go cash only. It is psychologically harder to spend cash than credit. Do not use your ATM card. If you do not have the cash for a purchase, you don't need it.

[5] Consult a financial planner or an accountant who specializes in small businesses to help you examine your overall financial requirements before starting your business.

[6] Select the right bank for your business and set up an account. Do *not* use the same bank for your personal account and your business account.

5

THINK LIKE A
BUSINESS OWNER

$$\left[\ \textit{Eleven months before you start}\ \right]$$

I once heard a man say, "You are one idea away from accomplishing anything you want." This is true. Entrepreneurs are visionaries. They see the big picture. They are leaders and innovators.

Sometimes, though, their visions are too broad and grandiose. They want a billion-dollar company like Google; a million-dollar business is not enough. Confidence in your ability and your product or service is essential, but the business vision must be realistic. You need to define that vision by your core services or products, your unique value proposition, the year-to-year revenue growth, and ultimately, how big you want the company to become. Your business vision is the articulation of the future of your company.

Visualizing Your Business

Let's start by defining a small business. The Small Business Association has established two widely used criteria:

- For most manufacturing and mining industries, the company can have a maximum of 500 employees
- For most nonmanufacturing industries, average annual receipts should not exceed $7 million

Go to *www.sba.gov* for more information about these standards.

Remember that you're starting a *small* business, in line with these standards. Don't let your vision run away with you. There will be plenty of opportunity for growth. While self-confidence is essential, you must be careful not to give the appearance of overconfidence.

If you're successful, you will attract mentors by being approachable and responsive. Some mentors will be clients; others will be angel investors or retired executives who may see something in you they want to nurture.

EMERSON'S essentials

There are plenty of people who have forgotten more than you know about business. *Use your attitude and excitement about your new enterprise to attract these people to work for you, support you, and do business with you.*

As a result of my experience working with thousands of small business owners to start and grow their businesses and talking to many successful entrepreneurs and small business experts, I have evolved seven essential principles of small business success. These elements are highlighted in detail throughout this book.

7 Essential Principles of Small Business Success

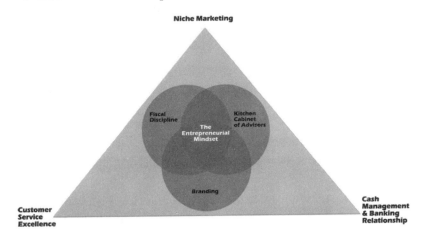

To start and run a successful small business, you must:

1. Have an entrepreneurial mindset.
2. Observe strict fiscal discipline
3. Form a kitchen cabinet of advisors to support you.
4. Have a defined brand identity and professional marketing collateral.
5. Focus on a niche market.
6. Provide excellent customer service.
7. Understand your cash position and carefully manage your banking relationship.

The Entrepreneurial Mindset

Why does one small business owner flourish while another one fails? Because successful entrepreneurs develop the right mindset. How you perceive your business and your life defines your reality.

- Business owners with an entrepreneurial mindset seek to stand out in the crowd.
- Successful small business owners keep a positive attitude.
- Entrepreneurs are willing to fail in order to eventually win. They understand that not every idea is a good one.
- Real entrepreneurs learn from failure and move on to the next big idea.

Each day we make hundreds of choices—from what to have for breakfast to what we're going to accomplish that day. The choices we make cause the results we experience. Your answers to the questions you ask yourself will determine the outcome of the day. To be a successful entrepreneur, you need not only to get the right answers; you need to make sure you're asking the right questions.

You must not be afraid of failure. There will be occasions when you are doing your best, but feel frustrated by a lack of progress in your business. Every entrepreneur goes through these difficult periods. I certainly have been there. Times like these are when you need to focus on the positive and maintain your optimism.

EMERSON'S essentials

We would not know good days if it were not for bad days. *When challenges come, figure out the lesson that you were supposed to learn, and move on.*

The key is to avoid negative thinking. To change the outcome of each day, you must change the questions you ask yourself. Try rephrasing your questions in a positive fashion. Rather than ask, "What can I do to avoid being late?", ask, "How can I make sure I am on time?" Make sure your questions are not keeping you from reaching your goals. More than 50 percent of business problems are well-disguised personal problems.

Losing the fear of failure and of making mistakes (provided, of course, that you learn from them) comes in part from a willingness to delegate. Beware of what I call "the cult of personality" business. Any company that kowtows to the owner's ego will ultimately fail.

I made this mistake in my first business. Everyone who called the office had to speak to me. My staff was scared to make a decision until they checked with me. My excessive control was keeping my business from growing.

You must hire smart people and empower them to make decisions, even if they are not the decisions you would make. Remember: It's not always about you. It is also about your family, your employees, and your customers.

Be a family-first entrepreneur. This means that you always have options, not obligations, and your family is always your number-one client. Don't let your business become your mistress. Try to compensate your family for the fact that, in the beginning of your business, you'll have to work very long hours.

Key to thinking like an entrepreneur is remaining focused. Here are some tips to motivate yourself:

- Develop a daily routine. Get up at the same time every day, take a shower, and exercise before you start work.
- Convert one room in the house into an office. Be aware that using a room with a bed makes naps inviting.

- Schedule breakfast meetings and early morning conference calls to get yourself going early.
- When you feel your energy getting low, take a walk around the block or get on a treadmill for thirty minutes.
- Avoid procrastination; perform follow-up activities right away. Send thank-you cards and e-mail follow-ups quickly.
- Ask a friend or fellow business owner to call or e-mail you to remind you about things you said you really needed to get done.

EMERSON'S essentials

Don't spend your work time on social networks unless there's a clear business-related reason. *If you open e-mail first thing each day or start replying right away to your LinkedIn, Twitter, and Facebook requests, you are working on someone else's agenda and not your own.*

Isolation is the enemy of entrepreneurship. You must not let the silence or boredom get to you. You may need to figure out how to change your work environment to get your work done. At the same time, you need to make sure you remain disciplined.

- Find a secondary workplace outside your home, e.g. a coffee shop, a bookstore, or the public library.
- Schedule your time. Plan when you will make sales calls, write checks, return calls, write blog posts, read e-mail, and open mail.
- Make an action list at the end of every day to drive work activities for the next day.

- Do not run errands until after 6 P.M. Politely inform those who ask that you are working.
- Do not make or accept personal calls until after 6 P.M. unless they're urgent. Explain to your friends and family about your work hours and make sure people respect them. "I need to call you back," works just fine to clear the line.
- Invest in a two-line telephone with speakerphone and a headset so that you can multitask.

EMERSON'S essentials

Your friends and family may not immediately make the connection that time is money for you. *When I first started in business, my mother would call to chat in the middle of the day. I felt isolated, so I would take her call, but it didn't benefit my business.*

Get a kitchen cabinet

Your Kitchen Cabinet is an unofficial board of directors for your business. It's a sounding board for your business ideas and challenges. The group should include a variety of people invested in your success, such as an existing entrepreneur, a mentor, lawyer, accountant, someone with a significant network and a generous spirit, and (if possible) a client. People who are already entrepreneurs or other business people are in a position to give you insight into what you need to do. As well, it is helpful to include a potential client in your back channel conversations. Clients can provide valuable insights into budget cycles, current pain-points, and other issues. Most importantly, they can introduce you to other potential customers.

Pace Yourself

Sometimes, when you look back over your day, you'll find yourself focusing on what you didn't get done. That's not helpful. There is rarely enough time in a day to get everything done. The best thing to do is to prioritize and pace yourself. Even a marathon runner has to rest and refresh to keep going.

The early days in business are the toughest. I believe Dr. Sanjay Gupta when he says we need to get seven to eight hours of sleep a night. But in the early days, while you are working your job and your business, a full night's sleep will be a luxury. Owning a business is great, but in the beginning it might own you. You have to fight the tendency to let the business take over your life.

In a way, owning a business is like being in a marriage. In business, as in marriage, you can get lax about the fundamentals, whether it's remembering to send flowers to your spouse or using monthly financial statements in your business.

Your business and your family will compete for your time and attention. Wherever you are, be present *there*. Do not be the parent on the ball field looking at your BlackBerry. The ups and down of balancing your life and your work will sometimes have you turning yourself into a pretzel. But when you get that first sale and when you make enough profit to pay yourself, sharing those moments with your family will be priceless.

Be a lifelong learner

Successful business owners constantly seek to sharpen their own knife. They keep learning and growing. They hire coaches, take seminars, enroll in executive-education programs, and approach life with the mindset that they learn something new every day. Even the interns can teach you something.

As you become a successful business owner, you can engage other people in your big dreams. Enthusiasm is contagious. If you believe in yourself, others will believe in you.

Goals and follow-up

Successful business owners are good talkers, but they're even better with follow-up. They strive for completion, not perfection. They embrace change by breaking out of their comfort zone, challenging themselves and others.

Visionary leaders inspire those around them because they've thought long and hard about where they want their business to go and how to get there. If you want to be like them, set Specific, Measurable, Attainable, Realistic, and Timely goals (SMART goals).

Once you've worked to make all these things part of your daily routine, you'll be thinking like a successful business owner.

EMERSON'S action steps

[1] List the seven essential habits of successful business owners and post it somewhere you can refer to it often.

[2] Remind yourself daily about the fundamentals of your business and your family life.

[3] Avoid negative thinking. Keep a positive attitude.

[4] Develop ways to motivate yourself and stay focused.

[5] Be a lifelong learner.

[6] Look for ways to inspire others.

[7] Develop a list of SMART goals.

6

CREATE YOUR
BUSINESS MODEL

$$\left[\textit{Ten months before you start} \right]$$

The next step on your timeline to becoming an entrepreneur is to refine your business concept. You must determine if your business idea is viable—that is, will it work as a business that will make money and eventually a profit. Ask yourself the following questions:

- Is there a need in the marketplace for my business?
- Who's the competition?
- What is my competitive advantage?
- How hard will it be to get my product to market?
- Is my product or service difficult to explain?
- Is my price point competitive?
- How will I meet the market demand?
- Is my business a product of "mother necessity?"

- Does my product or service have enough staying power?
- Does my business idea present long-term growth opportunities?

Is there a need in the marketplace for my business?

Creating a business without validating the market is like driving to a new city without a map or GPS system. It's a frustrating experience. You must make sure there's a real market you can sell to. Of course, you can also create a market need. In determining how to do this, quality market research is essential. If you can't afford primary research (i.e., talking directly to consumers), at least do thorough secondary research using the Internet, library, or industry reports. You can get free market research assistance from *www.score.org* and *www.export.gov/mrktresearch*.

Fee-Based Market Research Sites
- U.S. Department of Commerce: *www.stat-usa.gov/hometest. nsf?OpenDatabase*
- Hoover's: *www.hoovers.com*
- IBISWorld: *www.ibisworld.com*

Who's the competition?

Your product or service will always have competition. The need you've identified in the market is being met somehow. Whenever a new business owner walks up to me and starts talking about his business, I always ask about his market and his competition. If he tells me he has no competition, I politely end the conversation and walk away. Clearly he has not done his homework and is headed for disaster. Perceived lack of competition means one of three things:

1. There is no real market for your product

2. A monopoly controls the market so overwhelmingly that you can't even think of them as competition.

3. Your product does not exist. It's possible that you'll create an entirely new product (such as Apple did with the iPhone), but chances of that are slim for a self-funded small business.

In the event of heavy competition, beware of market saturation. There may be no room for a new player. If, in your neighborhood, drugstores are being built every few blocks—in some cases right across the street from each other—should you become an independent drugstore owner in your town? Probably not.

Determining your competition also requires some sort of market research. Who are your target customers? Teenagers? Seniors? Young mothers? Other small businesses? How many potential customers do you have? Is your target market growing or shrinking? Gauging demand is an inexact science and will often come down to your best guess.

What is your signature move?

You must have a defined competitive advantage. In what way are you more special than the competition? You must have distinct differences. Anyone can sell purses, tires, or provide marketing consulting—why should anyone buy from you? Your potential clients must find an exceptional benefit in your product or service to buy from you.

How hard is it to get your product to market?

Do you need money, manpower, manufacturing, and marketing to get your product to market? What technical expertise do you need to deliver the product and what distribution channel will you use to deliver your goods to the customer? Good businesses die every day due to lack of capital, or challenges with production or delivery.

Make sure you consider what it will *really* take to make your business dream a reality.

Is your product or service difficult to describe?

Sometimes you can put your business at a disadvantage by offering a product or service that requires so much explanation that potential customers are confused. No one should be confused about why they should buy a product. You may need to spend the first year or two in business educating people about your product. For example, it took some time for Apple to educate its consumers about how to use new features on their iPhones. A marketing campaign to make the market aware of your product is not impossible, but it can be very costly.

Is your price point competitive?

When considering a price point for your product, survey the competition. Your price must cover your costs, highlight the value you are providing the customer, and earn you a reasonable profit, but you must also be competitive. Test your pricing strategy before going with it. The marketplace will quickly tell you if your product's price is too high.

The wrong price will make a bad first impression. Often, you do not get a chance to make a second impression, so it's important to get this right. Realize that it's not always wise to be the cheapest offering. A salesperson for the top competitor to my multimedia company once told me that their company philosophy was to be the most expensive option in the market. It's a bold move, but if you spin it right, your customers will see real value in your offering.

Ultimately, pricing must be driven by economics. If you don't make a profit, what is the point in having a business in the first place?

How will you meet the market demand?

If you have the hottest Christmas toy for young children, your success will hinge on cashing in on the opportunity before the season ends. What sort of lead time do you need to meet the demand? It may take several months to get new inventory, which may be too late. There will be many up-front cash obligations to respond to this kind of business demand, so cash flow management is critical.

Is your business a product of "mother necessity"?

Finding an unmet need in the marketplace can be a great business strategy. Many new ideas and products are built on existing concepts but fill an underserved niche. For example, the post office has always delivered packages, but FedEx and UPS took that concept to the next level.

A successful business solves a problem or fulfills a want or a need. Your marketing strategy should always focus on customer needs— whether real or perceived. Lots of companies sell MP3 players, but Apple made the iPod a must-have.

Does your product or service have staying power?

Capitalizing on a fad is tricky business. Trends change quickly. If you plan to start a trend-driven business you must make sure you can enter it quickly while the fad is hot, and that your product has enough staying power for you to make your money and cash out before the market moves again.

Does your business idea present long-term growth opportunities?

Does your business idea present the possibility of line extensions in the future? If you're making homemade ice cream, will you create more flavors? If you make children's shoes, will you be able to expand into ladies' footwear?

Do you have the resources to constantly improve your product line? Will you create an expanded model in the future with more features? Is your product attractive to a global market? These are all questions that will determine how big your business can become.

Take Care of the Administrative Details

Once you've created a sound business concept—you know what you're going to make, how you're going to make it, and who you're going to make it for, you're ready to take the next step. You must create your business identity. That is, you must name the business and hire a lawyer to assist you in deciding on the appropriate legal structure. Then you must incorporate your new venture. This process is important in protecting your business from legal and competitive issues.

Naming your business

Naming your business is tough. You want the name to be catchy and memorable, but you also want to be taken seriously. Most importantly, you want a name that will work now and in the future.

Using your last name in naming your business is always a safe bet. The name of the business owner, whether by itself or with words describing the business, is a good option. Further, if you use your last name as the name of your business, you do not need to go to the trouble of filing a fictitious name form with your state government.

If, however, you decide to make up a name, you need to follow certain steps. It's best to find a name that encapsulates what you want people to think about your business. Examples of fictitious names include D4 Multimedia, Wal-Mart, and the Philadelphia Diamond Company.

Here are seven tips for naming your business.

1. Avoid a word that is hard to pronounce or spell. It annoys people, and it will be harder for Internet searchers to find your firm

2. Do not create a new word. It's never a good idea to have people scratching their heads wondering what a word means.

3. Do not use a word so common that it is easily forgettable. Always display your uniqueness to make your business memorable.

4. Avoid purposefully misspelled words. Do not add numbers, odd letters, or dashes in your business name to make it work on the Internet. Spell cat with a 'c,' not a 'k.'

5. Do an Internet search to check your business name. See if the URL is available. If someone is using your name, you have two choices: find another name or create the URL with "inc," "online," or "llc" after it. You can also create a URL that describes what you sell, e.g., bestpracticefundraising.com.

6. Do not use the name of your town. PNC Bank was once Pittsburgh National Bank. It changed because an increasing number of its customers were not from Pittsburgh. A name tied to your town can stifle your growth once you look outside your region for customers.

7. Once in business, if you realize that your name no longer works—change it. My first business was originally named Quintessence Entertainment, Inc. I finally changed it after the hundredth call asking if we booked music acts. A name change is a great PR hook and an excuse to hold a grand re-opening.

If you operate a business under a fictitious name, you must register in the state where you plan to do business. The purpose is to create a public record of who owns the business in order to protect the public from fraud. Registering your fictitious name *does not* provide your business with exclusive rights to use the name.

When you incorporate your business you earn the exclusive use of your corporate name in your state. Your corporate name may not be the same as, or confusingly similar, to the name of any other business. Depending on the state where you operate, there are penalties for failing to register a fictitious name.

Creating your legal structure

Next it is time to establish your legal business entity. You want to protect yourself legally while accomplishing your business goals. Your structure should reflect the kind of business you want and the size of your enterprise.

When it is time to incorporate your business, you will need an attorney. A small business attorney may charge between $500 and $1,500 to incorporate a business, depending on what is involved. You will need to consult with your attorney on which venture type will best serve you. Your accountant may also have a suggestion since different legal entities have different tax implications.

Once you are incorporated, your lawyer will provide you with a corporate kit, which may include articles of incorporation, bylaws, your first meeting minutes, any stock certificates issued, and your corporate seal. These records are critically important and should be kept in a safe place.

The most common forms of legal entities are sole proprietorship, partnership, S-corporation, limited liability company (LLC), and a corporation.

Sole proprietorship

In a sole proprietorship, there is no distinction between the owner and the company. You are personally responsible for the company's debts and more importantly, you can be held personally liable for any lawsuits filed against the company. The owner can report the business's profit or loss on personal income tax returns.

Partnership

In a partnership, two or more people come together jointly to own and operate a business. They share the same personal liability as the sole proprietorship. All aspects of running the business are shared among the partners, and each partner is personally liable for the business debt. Partnerships do not pay taxes but must file an informational tax return; each partner reports their financials from the business on their personal tax return.

Limited liability company (LLC)

A limited liability company (LLC) is a partnership that limits the liabilities of the business to the amount of investment by each partner. No personal assets are at risk. The LLC is generally considered a good option for small businesses because it combines the limited personal liability feature of a corporation with the tax advantages of a sole proprietorship. Owners can report the business financials on their personal tax returns or the LLC can elect to be taxed like a corporation. LLCs do not offer stock and are not required to observe corporate formalities, such as filing annual meeting minutes. Owners are called members, and the members manage the LLC.

Sub-chapter S corporation or S-corp

A sub-chapter S corporation provides limited liability and significant tax benefits for its owners. Profits are only reported on the business owner's personal tax return. The catch here is that the shareholder, if working for the company, and if there is a profit, must pay him/herself wages, and must meet standards of "reasonable compensation." In other words, you must pay yourself what you would have to pay someone to do your job. If you do not do this, the IRS can reclassify all of the earnings and profit as wages, and you will be liable for all of the payroll taxes on the total amount. S-corps involve a significant paper work burden and are limited to thirty-five stockholders.

Corporation

A corporation is a legal business entity that is separate from its owners. It can be private or publicly held. A corporation can be taxed, it can be sued, and it can enter into contractual agreements. The owners of a corporation are its shareholders. The shareholders elect a board of directors to oversee the major policies and decisions. The corporation has a life of its own and does not dissolve when ownership changes.

Which of these legal structures you choose depends on what you're selling, the size of your company, your investors' preferences, and other key factors.

EMERSON'S action steps

[1] Determine if your business idea is viable. Answer the Who, What, Where, When, Why and How, of your business concept:

WHO is your target market?
WHAT business are you in?
WHERE will you sell it?
WHEN will you make a profit?
WHY should anyone buy from you?
HOW will you promote it?

[2] Think long and hard about your business name.

[3] Consult an attorney about the right way to incorporate your business.

7

Line Up a Lawyer and an Accountant

[*Ten months before you start*]

As the previous chapter made clear, two of the most important resources your business will need are legal and financial advice. You always need to make sure you are operating legally. You also need to make sure your business model is financially viable. A lawyer can advise you on your business incorporation, contracts, lease agreements, intellectual property protection, and other elements critical to your business. An accountant or bookkeeper will help you develop your initial financial projections, budgets, track revenues and expenses monthly, set up your accounting software, and keep you on top of your tax liabilities.

How to Hire An Attorney

When it is time to incorporate your business, you need to engage an attorney. She will advise you how to incorporate your business. She will also advise you whether you will need to secure patents, trademarks, or copyrights on your logo, slogan, systems, written materials, or products. Your attorney should review any contracts you are asked to sign, especially any leases, franchise agreements, or loan documents. The lawyer should also draft the contract that you will use for your customers to engage services, any employment contracts, and your noncompete and nondisclosure agreements that all employees and strategic partners should sign.

It's best to hire a lawyer who has experience with small businesses, but you also want to make sure that your business consultant is responsive and has time for you. If you are considering purchasing a business or buying into a franchise, look for a lawyer who specializes in franchise agreements.

EMERSON'S essentials

You should feel comfortable with your lawyer and not intimidated. *Look for experts who are smart, collaborative, informative, and, most of all, will listen to you. I also like to look for vendors who can help get more business.*

If you select a lawyer from a large law firm, you may not get the one-on-one attention you may need as a start-up business, and you are guaranteed to get a big bill.

Whoever you decide to use, check their qualifications. You can review the attorney's credentials on your state bar's website or use *www.martindale.com*. Make sure that the attorney is licensed and admitted to practice before the courts in your state. The state bar records will also inform you if the attorney has ever been reprimanded or involved in any illegal activity. Ask for referrals. Many small business development centers have partnerships with the law schools and the local bar association to offer pro-bono advice to start-up businesses. When selecting an attorney, interview at least three candidates, ask them for small-business references, and make sure that you check them.

Here are some questions for a potential lawyer:

- Do I need to provide a large retainer to get started?
- What is your fee schedule for routine and nonroutine services?
- Will you provide itemized bills?
- What is your typical response time?
- What is the best way to reach you?
- Have you worked with any businesses in my industry?
- Can you provide three small-business references?
- Can you give me an example of how you have helped clients secure business opportunities?
- Can I call you on any legal problem?

Get ready for business taxes

Once you are incorporated, you must obtain an Employer Identification Number (EIN) from the Internal Revenue Service. The number is also known as a Federal Tax ID Number and identifies a business on a tax return. You will also need an EIN number to open a business bank account. If you are a sole proprietor with no employees you do not need an EIN number. You should use your social security number.

You need to get an EIN number if you:

- Have a payroll,
- Have a SEP IRA or self-employed retirement plan,

- Incorporate your business, or
- File any employment, excise, fiduciary, or alcohol, tobacco, and firearms tax returns.

You can secure the number easily at *www.irs.gov.*

How to Hire an Accountant

The next critical resource you will need is a good accountant. There are three levels of accounting experts you can hire: a bookkeeper, an accountant, and a certified public accountant (CPA). The main differences between these providers are their hourly rates and the level of services they provide to small business owners.

A Bookkeeper will set up your accounting software and enter receipts and invoices into your software weekly or monthly, handle payroll data and quarterly taxes, and create your monthly financial statements (income statements, balance sheets, cash flow statements.) Bookkeepers are primarily accounting clerks responsible for recording accounting transactions and reconciling your bank statements. Bookkeepers typically do not prepare business tax returns. They also may not have the knowledge to help analyze your financial position. They may have two- or four-year business or accounting college degrees or they may just have on-the-job training.

An Accountant is qualified to handle the day-to-day bookkeeping needs of your company. He will set up your accounting software, accounts payable and accounts receivable charts, prepare payroll data and reporting requirements, and prepare other monthly financial statements.

Accountants can also prepare business taxes. Accountants generally have college degrees and are trained to interpret and analyze financial data. They have a higher skill level and a higher hourly rate than bookkeepers.

A Certified Public Accountant (CPA) is an accountant who has passed a rigorous state examination. Only CPAs can certify an audit. CPAs provide all levels of accounting and consulting services and prepare tax returns. CPAs also provide tax planning and are highly qualified experts in accounting. As such, they are expensive.

You want an accountant who has experience will small businesses and your industry. You also need to make sure that your business consultant is patient and responsive because you may have a lot of questions starting out. Your accountant should be easy to talk to and good at explaining your accounting software as well as unfamiliar terms such as depreciation, chart of accounts, cost of goods sold, and balance sheets. My preference is a smaller accounting firm or a solo practice over a large accounting firm because costs are generally lower. Shop around until you find the right fit. New tax laws are passed every year, so your tax professional may not be the same person who does your monthly accounting and reconciliation of your accounts.

Here's a list of questions that you should ask a candidate you are considering:

- What accounting software do you use?
- Do you provide software set-up?
- Do you provide monthly bookkeeping or do you have a preferred list of vendors we should use?
- What is your hourly rate?
- Will you prepare a contract with a set monthly fee?

- Can you provide three small-business references?
- Do you work onsite at the client location?
- Do you work with many start-up businesses?
- What industries do you specialize in?
- Have you worked with any businesses in my industry?
- Do you also prepare business taxes?

One of the first things your accountant will need to do is help you create your operating budget and sales projections for your business plan. I'll discuss this more in Chapter 10.

Your accountant will recommend the kind of accounting software you should purchase. If you are comfortable with computers, there are a wide variety of computer programs on the market to help you manage your accounting, including: QuickBooks Pro, Small Business Manager, Peachtree Complete Accounting, and Simply Accounting. Ask your accountant which software makes the most sense for your business. You'll find an exhaustive list of accounting software options at *www.accountingsoftware411.com*. Many programs offer a free thirty-day trial use as well.

EMERSON'S essentials

Payroll taxes are very complicated and confusing. *You do not want to make a mistake. You can get in trouble quicker for not paying payroll taxes than you can for not paying income taxes.*

None of the programs will work, however, if you do not input your information on a regular basis. Use your accounting software to track all sales, invoices, receipts, and any payroll. You should also keep physical copies of all receipts, invoices, and cancelled checks. It's a good habit to keep a notebook in your car to track your business mileage. Some people attach a little notepad to their dashboard.

Consult with your accountant to learn about the various state and local tax issues for your business. These issues include potential deductions and any requirements for paying estimated taxes, or hiring employees. If you are going to have full-time employees, it may make more sense to engage a payroll service.

Before you start a business, be sure to check the zoning restrictions in your area, particularly if you plan to be home-based. There could be possible restrictions in your neighborhood on the kind of business you intend to run. Be sure to secure any business licenses required to operate your business.

Sales Taxes

Here are some basic rules for determining if you are required to charge sales tax on your products or services.

Manufacturing sales are tax-exempt. If your company processes a product, then resells it in a different form, you are considered a manufacturer. Anything that is directly used in the manufacturing process is considered tax-exempt in most states. This doesn't mean that everything used in your business is tax-exempt; it only applies to the products that actually are used to develop your finished goods. For example, if you manufacture DVDs, all of the blank DVDs, labels, ink, and shrink wrap materials used to produce the DVDs are tax-exempt, but the packaging materials to ship the product are not.

Casual sales are tax-exempt. If you have a garage sale in your neighborhood, you do not need to collect sales taxes. But if you regularly sell antiques out of your house to your neighbors, you are running a business. Casual sales do not take place more than twice a year.

Computers may be tax-exempt. In some states, computers and accessories used in your business operations are tax-exempt. However, the computers must be used directly to manufacture finished goods. Technology companies can especially benefit from this. Ask your accountant to verify this before claiming this exemption.

Internet entrepreneurs pay sales tax too. You only charge sales taxes when you ship a product to a state where you have a physical presence or a license to do business.

Some services may be tax-exempt. Ask you accountant to clarify your state's sales-tax code. Every state has a list of services that are taxable. If your business service is not listed, breathe easy: your company is tax-exempt.

EMERSON'S experience

Your business may be considered tax-exempt based on its location. Pennsylvania's Keystone Opportunity Zones program, for example, eliminates certain taxes for businesses that locate in certain qualified areas. Check with your county or look on your state's website for community and economic development to find these programs.

My first business was located in a Keystone Opportunity Zone. For five years we enjoyed tax-exempt status.

EMERSON'S action steps

[1] Hire a small-business lawyer to handle the initial processes of establishing your business. Get a specialist if you are dealing with a complex issue like a franchise agreement.

[2] Seek out an accountant who works with small businesses and has experience in your industry.

[3] Make sure you understand the specific sales tax requirements in your state.

[4] Stay on top of your tax liabilities. Entrepreneurs are always susceptible to an audit by the IRS.

Part II

GET SET!

Sunday	Monday	Tuesday	Wednesday	Thursday	Friday	Saturday
				1	2	3
4	5	6	7	8	9	10
11	12	13	14	15	16	17
18	19	20	21	22	23	24
25	26	27	28	29	30	31

8

NICHE TO GET RICH!

$$\left[\ \textit{Nine months before you start}\ \right]$$

It certainly has a nice ring to it. Who doesn't want to get rich? But what the heck is a niche? Webster's Business Dictionary defines a niche as a "particular market or specialty area where a company finds it profitable to concentrate its efforts. Niche marketing offers a concentration of clients in an area of limited competition." The key words here are "concentration of clients" and "limited competition"—sweet words for the budding entrepreneur.

A "market niche" can be a specific geographic area, such the mid-Atlantic region, a specialty industry such as sugar-free desserts, ethnic or age groups such a Generation X-ers, or any other group of people with certain common characteristics, such as people who do not own cars. Niche businesses can also position themselves as specialists, charge more, and generate higher profit margins.

Find Your Dream Niche

A niche can be anywhere:

- Under (or on) your nose (think Breathe Right strips for people who snore)
- Cyberspace (where eBay, Amazon, and YouTube, among others, have generated millions of dollars)

Sometimes a niche is something no one else does (a CPA friend of mine specializes in restaurant accounting) or something no one wants to do (picking up dog poop, a small business that generates $100,000 per year). Sometimes a niche can be created by improving a common product already on the market (the Swiffer, the sleek hand duster, or Splenda, the sugar substitute). A business that focuses on addressing an unmet need can be a niche business too. Think Zipcar, a car-sharing business for people with an occasional need for wheels.

Your task in this chapter is finding or inventing your niche. Here are some general guidelines:

Go with what you know. Bob spent many years in the tow truck business. He was located close to a major turnpike, and the work was very competitive. In an effort to find a niche, he decided to buy a tow truck that could tow and lift big rigs. There were no competitors within fifty miles, and his revenues rose 50 percent the first year. He was an expert in towing and used his skills to specialize.

Work for a business like the one you plan to start. As you gain experience in a field, you may see a niche that your employer is ignoring. You can also learn what you should and should not do in *your* business. You will be far smarter about suppliers, customer requirements, costs, and pitfalls related to your potential business. You may also gain access to other markets that you never considered.

EMERSON'S experience

I have a friend who worked for a major conglomerate early in his career. As a product manager, he saw an opportunity for his business to expand their services into a product area that would generate an additional $25 million in revenue a year.

He researched the market, developed the business plan, and presented the business case to his superiors. In the end, the company passed on the opportunity, claiming that $25 million in revenue was not significant enough to dedicate the resources to pursue the opportunity.

My friend realized that if they didn't want to pursue it, he could. So he worked for that business unit another nine months, then quit to start his firm. He has not hit $25 million yet, but he is closing in on it.

Look for "you must be kidding" opportunities. The enterprising entrepreneur can find a pot of gold in everything from bathroom maintenance services, pest control, window washing, maintaining septic systems, to building a pet-sitting business. Beauty is in the eye of the beholder, and what some would see as unattractive jobs, others see as a potential mint. Typically, if you pursue an "ugly" business, you can bet that the competitors will be few and the potential unlimited.

Turn a hobby into a money machine. Stories abound about cookie makers (Famous Amos, Mrs. Fields, etc.) who went from the kitchen to national enterprises because they were tuned into America's taste buds. In my area, a local toy store grew out of the owner's affection for model trains. He now specializes in selling unique toy trains nationwide using the Internet.

Invent something. Mother Necessity is always looking for solutions to problems. The Butler Bag, PedEgg, plastic garbage bags, the Jet Ski, and WD-40 are just a few of the many products created by inventors who made a niche where none existed before. A great example: my friend Julia Rhodes realized that children need more flexible writing environments. She invented hand-held dry erase boards, which she called KleenSlate Concepts, for children and schools. She also created a line of dry erase markers with the felt eraser tip attached to the marker.

EMERSON'S essentials

The best thing you can do for your business venture is know your customers intimately. *That means spending time talking to them, asking them questions, studying professional literature about them, and watching their spending habits in regards to your business.*

She also promoted her product in a unique way. She made clothes for herself from her product and walked around trade shows writing on herself and then erasing it. Her stunts got her noticed by retailers and even got her a spot on the inventors showcase on *The Tonight Show with Jay Leno*. Her products are now sold through major office supply stores, national supply catalogs, and retail school supply chains nationwide.

If you can create an improvement that the public can embrace, congratulations! You are now a niche business owner.

Your Approach to Niche Marketing

The more focused you are on who your customer is, where they shop, where they live, how often they buy things, what their values are, and what their struggles are, the easier it is to sell to them. For example, imagine you offer a product for working mothers with children under five years old. You could advertise on easy listening radio stations, which many women typically play at work. You can also advertise in *Parenting* or *Working Mother* magazines or on such websites targeting working mothers. By carefully defining your customer you reduce the risk of wasting money, and your marketing dollars will go a lot further. If you want to catch a fish, you have to go where hungry fish are swimming.

EMERSON'S experience

My friend Jen Groover is the creator of the Butler Bag. She got the idea to redesign women's handbags after a nightmare experience in a grocery store. She was in the checkout line with a screaming child on each hip trying to find her wallet to pay for her groceries. She looked down into her bottomless pit of a handbag and couldn't see her wallet. At home later that day she realized that if purses had compartments, it would be easier to find things in them. She developed her prototype using the utensil caddy from her dishwasher. Today, the Butler Bag is a multimillion-dollar company and the fastest-growing brand in the handbag industry.

Use the Internet to go deeper into your market. I know a lawyer who advertises his practice on a DUI website. On his own website, he has published articles and a blog about criminal law and DUI. He has researched the key words people used to search for help with DUI arrests and has made sure to use those key words in his blog posts.

You can use the web to establish your niche brand at the same time you develop new ways to satisfy existing demand. Why? Because something that's different invites attention on the web.

Another method of differentiation is to focus on developing greater product value. You can accomplish this by manipulating price or increasing the perceived worth of your product or service through aggressive branding. For example, you might affiliate your product with a celebrity/personality or authority who occupies your niche. The skin-care company Proactive promoted its line of products to relieve acne by getting an endorsement from several actresses and a former Miss USA—for all of whom clear skin is essential.

EMERSON'S essentials

Finding the right niche for your business means you can spend more time generating business and less time looking for the market. *In a niche business, you know where your customers live, shop, and work, so that makes it easier to find them. You can concentrate on generating a message and value proposition that appeals to them.*

Testing Your Niche

Before settling on your niche, test it to make sure a business aimed at it will be viable. There are several ways you can do this.

If a real niche exists, chances are you'll find media targeting it. Look for blogs, magazines, trade journals, newspapers, and other media aimed at your customer base.

There is a big difference between magazine "circulation" and "readership." What matters to you are circulation numbers for media aimed at your intended niche. "Readership" is a meaningless number. Find out the circulation of magazines aimed at your niche. This will tell you something about the size of the market.

Buy a mailing list. Niche-specific publications will sometimes rent you their mailing lists for a one-time use fee. If you rent a set of names, do not attempt to reuse the list. Publications always place trace names in the list that will alert them to your violation of the usage terms.

You can usually sort the names on the list by variables such as zip code, gender, income, etc. If you are testing a niche market, confine your first mailing to zip codes in your general area. Follow-up will be much easier and less costly.

For other mailing lists, contact a "list broker" or a direct-mail house in your area. Define your target market and the broker will find an appropriate list for you.

Surveys and focus groups can indicate whether your product or service has a market. Ask people if and why they might buy what you are selling. Test a few price points so potential customers can tell you what it's worth to them. If the product is tangible, let them examine and use it.

As part of your market research, buy products from your competitors. Study their sales process and delivery systems. How can you improve on them and make your customers' experience better?

Remember that you must fulfill a *unique need*. If you understand what your potential audience needs, you can customize products or services specifically for them—either to relieve the pain caused by a problem or to give them pleasure.

People like options. Consider the different features you may be able to offer.

If you can afford it, run a test ad in a newspaper, on TV, or radio to gauge public interest in what you are selling. If you get a good response, follow up with a survey questionnaire attached to a product registration card to get more information on who might buy your product.

When approaching a new market niche, it's important to be clear about the benefit you are offering and to speak the language of your customer. Are you talking to nurses or landscapers or HVAC retailers? They all have different issues and communicate using a lot of industry-specific language. In other words, you need to sound like your target market and be prepared to communicate with them as an insider, not an outsider.

Do your homework

I am a big fan of cheap wisdom. Go to the library. Search the Internet. Read, research, do your "due diligence," check costs, competition, and get a feel for the size and viability of your target niche market. The time you spend up-front in gaining knowledge will pay huge returns later.

Stay focused

Distractions from your core niche are everywhere. If your specialty is repairing European foreign cars, avoid—at least initially—branching out into domestic vehicles. Broadening your focus is dangerous because it takes you away from your chosen niche, one that you've determined will be the driving force behind your business. The more time it takes you to do an inspection on a Ford Taurus, the less time you are performing your more profitable work on Volvos and Audis. You cannot be all things to all people. Pick your place and build your business there.

EMERSON'S essentials

Be known for something. *People respect expert knowledge. The more you know, the better your expertise, and the stronger your chances of success.*

Is It a Money Maker?

Last, but not least, how much money is in your market niche? What is its buying power? How much do your target consumers spend in your industry? And how much of the market share do you need to start making a profit?

The answers to some of these questions can be found by examining online sources, companies' annual reports, and by reading business publications such as *BusinessWeek, Small Business,* and *The Wall Street Journal.* Dig in and do the research!

Now that you've decided on your niche, you can begin to get into the details of how you will market to your customers. In the next chapter, we'll develop the plan's contents and see how important it is in the grand scheme of things.

EMERSON'S action steps

[1] Define your niche market.

[2] Do the necessary market research to know your customers intimately.

[3] Study the competition and their operations and products.

[4] Test your potential target market through online surveys, focus groups, ads, and mailings.

9

Marketing 101: Eyeing Who's Buying

$$\left[\ \textit{Nine months before you start}\ \right]$$

You will notice that this book asks you to develop the marketing plan before the business plan. I do it this way, so that you do not waste time. If you do not know who's buying and why they should buy from your business, you should not waste your time writing a business plan. If you get stuck trying to validate your market opportunity, however, you will know not to quit your job and start a business.

The cornerstone of your new business should be your marketing plan. *Your marketing plan is the foundation upon which your business plan is built.* A solid marketing plan includes everything from the product offerings or core services, number and type of potential customers, to pricing, competition, sales, and much more.

Why such detail? It is much easier and cheaper to do your homework before you open your doors than to scramble after the business is operating. A good marketing plan forces you to think about your business's growth potential and the amount of profit you will generate.

Let's define some basic marketing terms:

Marketing—Marketing is anything you do to generate sales. It creates awareness that a product or service exists. Marketing presents products or services in ways that make them desirable.

Market research—This tells you who could buy your product, why they would buy it, and helps you estimate how many people are potential customers for both the long- and short-term. It helps you decide how to reach customers and influences your advertising approach.

Advertising—Advertising is a tactic of marketing. It calls attention to a product or service in order to build awareness and make a sale. Brand messaging is a critical element of advertising.

Sales—The job of sales is to convince the customer to purchase your product or service. Sales activities include person-to-person selling, e-mail selling, direct mail, promotions and discounts, trade show displays, telemarketing, and network marketing. Your financial projections are built on projected sales.

Profits—Profits are how much money you make from sales after deducting all of your costs of doing business. Your direct and indirect costs, together with market research, will dictate your pricing. From the start, you need to make sure you are making enough profit to stay in business.

Phillip Kotler, a legendary name in academic marketing circles, defines marketing as "human activity directed at satisfying needs and wants through exchange processes." I define marketing a bit more simply as, "activities and programs focused on who's buying and why."

Marketing answers the questions: Who are your target customers? How will you reach the customers? What product benefits will appeal to the market? *The only way to impact the selling process is to understand the customer and the marketplace.* No matter how good your product, without a basic understanding of how to market your goods or services, you will have a tough time generating sales.

Marketing versus advertising

Small business owners sometimes confuse marketing and advertising. They're two very different, though related, things. I like to think of marketing as anything you do to generate sales. Advertising is a marketing tactic. It's paid, public, nonpersonal communication about your product or service designed to generate sales and brand awareness. It's also usually the most expensive element of any marketing strategy. Memorable advertising possesses the strength needed to accomplish your sales objectives.

Think of marketing as a tool belt. Advertising is the hammer; public relations is the utility knife; social media is the wrench, and market research is the screwdriver. There are many other tools on the tool belt, but those are the four you reach for most often.

Your marketing plan brings together your understanding of the market, your customer, your competition, and your pricing. From these, it generates a strategic and tactical approach to your product and a marketing budget to support this approach. Your plan will also need to delineate your positioning in the market place, your niche focus, value proposition and competitive advantage. In other words, your marketing plan clarifies who your customer is and why they should buy from you.

If you have been selling for a long time, you may be very comfortable with marketing and think you have a clear idea of your market. Remember, though, it is always dangerous to make assumptions about the needs and wants of your customers.

EMERSON'S essentials

You must stay in communication with your core customers. *Go out and meet with them a few times a year. Do not just send them an invoice. Spend some time with them.*

The Four Ps of Your Marketing Plan

The four P's of marketing are tools to help you create sales efficiency. The goal is to make as many highly profitable sales as possible. Understanding what you need to maximize both profits and sales is the key to developing an effective marketing plan. The four Ps should be an important section of your plan.

The good news is that much of the information you need to develop a plan is free or low cost. Spend time on the Internet, go to the library, subscribe to industry publications, join trade organizations, contact the local Chamber of Commerce, read government publications, and talk to potential customers. These are great sources of information.

Let's examine each of the four Ps.

■ **Product**—Describe the product or service you will offer, including branding, size, options, quality, warranties, and packaging. Explain how the product will meet client needs, what geographic area will be served, what are the features and benefits of that product or service, and what is your competitive edge. Explain how it will be manufactured or performed.

- **Placement**—Explain how the product/service will be delivered. Describe the distribution channels and the physical facilities (e.g., warehouse, garage, fulfillment house, office space, strategic alliance facility or other area) needed for the movement of the product from manufacturing to the hands of the consumer.
- **Promotion**—Develop a mix of marketing activities. Outline what advertising channels you'll use to get the word out, i.e., Internet, flyers, magazines, newspapers, direct mail, telemarketing, radio, and television. Lay out your public relations strategy. Review your personal and business networks.
- **Price**—Decide what the market will pay. Pricing strategy is all about pricing your product or service for your different target markets. Determine the list price, discounts, wholesale allowances, markdowns, payment periods, and credit terms. Based on positioning, decide if your product will have premium or discount pricing.

EMERSON'S essentials

Small businesses, particularly start-ups, should not try to compete on price. *That is a losing proposition. A large competitor can undercut your price. Your better bet is to compete on quality, quick turn-around, or customer service.*

The Next Step

Now that you've got the four Ps in place, you need to add some elements to the plan:

1. Validate the market
2. Define your target customer
3. Create customer value
4. Identify your competitors and how you plan to deal with them
5. Define your marketing tactics
6. Determine your marketing budget

Validate the Market

How large is the market locally, nationally, and globally? How often do people buy your type of product? How many customers are "in market" at any given time? Will your customers buy daily, weekly, monthly, annually, or every five to ten years?

EMERSON'S essentials

What is your competitive advantage? *You must define what makes you special to your customers. If you don't know, ask the customer!*

Define Your Customer

Income? Location? Age? Size? Education? Profession? Can you see the face of your customer? Remember, the better you know your customer, the better your chances of making the sale. Keep in mind that your competition is targeting the same people you are and your message can easily get lost in advertising clutter and spam.

Create Customer Value

Start by identifying what qualities your customers value most and least about your service. You must build your marketing strategy on the customers' perception of your product's value to them. This approach is called WIIFM or What's in it for me? It's very important to keep your marketing plan customer-focused.

Define Your Marketing Tactics

There are a number of marketing tactics you should consider, but keep in mind that as a small business, particularly with a niche market, it doesn't make much sense to go big and expensive. Fortunately, a lot of marketing tactics these days take a relatively cheap approach:

> **Viral marketing**—In the age of social media, this may be the most powerful marketing tool in business. In social media it's all about give to get. The goal is to provide value to build relationships, which will "create buzz," so that people pass your marketing message on to anyone in their personal network. It is very different from direct selling. Openly advertising or pushing a business on social networking sites without providing value first is generally frowned upon. If someone has a great customer experience, they can voluntarily become ambassadors for your brand.

If I find out about a great new hair salon, I can get on Twitter and let my 8,000 followers in on it. If the new salon sends me a follow-up e-mail with a link to their website, they make it easier for me to spread the word. And if the salon offers me a discount for recommending friends, they give me an incentive to spread their message.

Social media sites such as YouTube are great for spreading the word about your product or service, but you must make sure you have a strong call to action. Otherwise you'll have a popular video on

YouTube and very little business. Your real goal is not to talk about your business yourself, but to *get your customers to do it.*

Online Marketing—Investing in a website is a must for any small business. In this Internet-focused age, your website is more important than hard copy marketing materials.

One of the keys to successful Internet marketing is being able to immediately solve the client's problem on your home page. Try not to make the customer search for product or support information. Include an e-commerce function, so your customer can easily pay for purchases. Be careful not to focus too much on "wow" features like music audio introductions or flash animation. There's more detail about this in Chapter 13.

EMERSON'S essentials

People will check out your website before they call you to place an order. *Make sure your site is user-friendly, and that all the links are working.*

E-mail marketing—E-mail marketing is all about communicating with past, current, and potential customers on a regular basis. Building a strong list of e-mail addresses is the foundation of any e-mail marketing campaign. Your website should have at least three to five list-building activities. Once you have a list you should regularly send out e-newsletters, special offers, sale announcements, special reports, membership programs, and reminders about your products and services. For how to build a strong e-mail list, read Chapter 13.

Event marketing—Attending industry trade shows is a great way to build potential long-term relationships. Purchasing a booth where you can demonstrate your product can give you a good return on investment. Just be careful that you attend trade shows focused on your target market. The first year you attend any trade show, go as an attendee. If the crowd is great, you can get a booth the following year.

A trade show starts the clock on your sales cycle. You never know when a contact can turn into a customer. Quality follow-up is key to this kind of sale. You can also consider buying ads in program books at high-profile events. You might sponsor a contest, host a tournament, or underwrite a public service program. Just make sure you quantify the upside before committing your limited resources.

Street marketing—Fliers, handbills, and posters can be real attention-getters if tied to some promotional offering that has a time constraint. Capitalizing on high-traffic places and events like hair salons and barber shops, churches, conventions, and concerts can be a cost-effective way to raise your visibility.

Set Your Marketing Budget

Now that you've decided on your overall marketing strategy and what specific tactics you're going to implement, you need to budget what you can spend on marketing. You must be realistic and prioritize your resources. It would be great to do everything you want to, but you need to decide how much you can devote to marketing activities and stick to that number.

Keep in mind that sales and marketing have to compliment each other. Your marketing activities must be focused to generate the number of sales leads that you need to meet your financial projections.

How to develop your marketing budget

1. Compare marketing costs to the number of sales you need to generate to determine the cost of marketing per customer.
2. Create methods to measure the return on investment of your marketing campaigns. You need to realize the highest possible rate of return on each marketing dollar spent.
3. Plan your marketing programs based on how many sales you need to generate. Calculate the rate at which you can convert leads into sales, and then determine what resources you'll need to generate that number of new leads.
4. Track your marketing programs closely and make them flexible enough to change with market conditions.
5. Allocate funding for future marketing efforts to continue to attract customers.

It's important that you are as accurate as possible in your estimation of the costs of various marketing tactics. There's nothing worse than finding out at the last minute that you don't have the money for some important marketing initiative.

Execution Is Key

Marketing plans are at the heart of small business success, but they are not worth the paper they are written on if they are not properly executed. The biggest mistake small business owners make with their marketing plans is losing focus.

Sometimes this can happen because you don't stick to the target market. Another common mistake is inconsistent messaging (e.g., your website and your brochures have different branding messages).

EMERSON'S essentials

Be sure, when you're setting up your business, to arrange to process credit cards. *So much business is done via credit card these days that even if you're selling something very inexpensive and running your business out of your home office, not accepting credit cards will cut you off from a lot of potential revenue.*

A third error is lack of discipline in implementation. This shows itself in small things as well as in big ones. If you send a letter that says you are going to follow up with a call in ten days, you'd better do it. Your customer will remember if you don't.

Developing a Sales Strategy

You have done your marketing homework. You've got your strategies and tactics, and you've compiled your budget. Now you need to create a plan for how to sell to your customers. A good marketing plan helps to raise customer awareness about who your company is and what it sells. It also helps you to understand who's buying your product and why, and the benefits you offer. To get customers to buy you must ask for the business. That's where your selling strategy comes in.

There are several ways you can sell your product or service, none of which exclude any others.

Direct sales—You or your salespeople pitch the customer on your service or product, write the order, and take payment. This can be door-to-door, like Mary Kay and Avon, or at your own retail location.

Direct mail order—Customers view products online or in a catalog and call in the order by phone. They provide a credit card for payment or pay cash on delivery, and you mail the goods to them.

Internet—Customers order via an online store on your website. Customers can place an order over a secured connection like Authorize.net, VeriSign, or Paypal. You can set up your own e-commerce site using a shopping cart system such as 1shoppingcart.com, and merchant services account to accept payments directly.

Indirect sales—You can use jobbers, wholesalers, or retail outlets to distribute your product to customers. A jobber is an intermediary who buys excess merchandise at prices typically 20–70 percent below wholesale and sells it at a discount either directly to customers or to a retail outlet. Jobbers supply stores like Value City, Burlington Coat Factory, and Big Lots. For other retail outlets, the decision to carry your product will be made by a buyer, who will decide if your product has sales potential and where in the store it should be displayed.

Each of these sales channels has a cost and varies in efficiency. Determine how your target customer likes to purchase goods, and use that method to start. Often product price and your manufacturing system will affect which channel you use, but the customer is the ultimate decision-maker on purchasing preferences.

EMERSON'S action steps

[1] Identify the four Ps: Product, Placement, Promotion, and Price

[2] Identify your target customer, the marketing tactics you will use to reach him or her, and set your marketing budget.

[3] Set a sales strategy that fits your customers' established buying patterns.

10

EVERY BUSINESS
NEEDS A PLAN

$$\left[\; \textit{Eight months before you start} \;\right]$$

One of my mentors, Morris Anderson, says, "A ship without a compass will have a tough time navigating." And for the same reason, any small business, whether it has a million-dollar launch or just a few hundred dollars to get started, needs a business plan. Your business plan is the road map for reaching your future business destination. It does not have to be complex; it can be as minimal as ten pages or as long as forty-five pages or so. The length of the plan is not the issue; it's the quality of the strategy outlined in the plan that really counts. Whether you start a small lawn-care service or a major manufacturing firm with 100 employees, your plan needs to be well researched and have reasonable financial projections. All businesses need the same thing—a business plan that the owner can follow to accomplish his or her long-term goals.

Writing a business plan is a good exercise. It will force you to describe the fundamental elements of your business: what business you are in, why you are in it, what you hope to accomplish, and what the growth potential is in your market. The plan must also describe the availability of skilled labor necessary to meet your company needs, and how you will generate additional start-up capital. It will help you think through how you will actually run your business. If you follow the twelve-month planning process laid out in this book, you will accomplish the following:

- Establish a clear connection between your business strategy and your marketing plan
- Identify the latest socio-economic data and industry trends
- Develop a clear rationale for the marketing strategy
- Highlight the experience and management skills of the business owner(s)
- Produce a capacity building plan to accommodate growing operations
- Develop an operating budget and realistic financial projections

There are three main uses for a business plan: communication, management, and planning.

1. As a communication tool, the business plan helps the owner to:

- Attract investment capital
- Secure loans
- Attract employees
- Attract strategic business partners
- Demonstrate profitability
- Demonstrate due diligence

2. As a management tool, the business plan helps the owner to:

- Track, monitor, and evaluate progress
- Modify strategy as knowledge and experience are gained
- Establish timelines and milestones
- Compare projections to actual accomplishments

3. As a planning tool, the business plan helps the owner to:

- Advance through the phases of business development
- Help identify roadblocks and obstacles
- Establish alternative plans

EMERSON'S essentials

People spend more time planning their vacation than they do planning how to run their small business. *The business plan is your road map to get you from where you are to where you want to be as a business owner.*

What's in a Business Plan?

The components of the plan include:

- Cover Page
- Executive Summary
- Business Description
- Market Analysis
- Marketing Plan
- Operations Plan

- The Management Team
- Intellectual Property Strategy
- Financial Projections

Cover page

This is the first page of the business plan. It should include the date, name of the business, the names of all business owners, and contact information for the key contact person. The cover page should also be marked confidential. Your plan is private, and you should not show it to just anyone. It contains information about your strategies, tactics, and projected revenues that your competitors would like to know. Be careful how widely you circulate it.

The executive summary

This should be written after the document is complete. The executive summary gives an overview of the important aspects of your business. It provides a brief description of the product or service and generates interest in your business idea. It clarifies the size of the market opportunity, and communicates your marketing strategy and your unique selling position in the marketplace. It summarizes how much money you will need to start or grow and estimates your year-over-year expected profitability. It should include a paragraph or two on each section of the business plan. It should not be more than two pages.

The business description

This is the explanation of your business idea. It should be brief, well thought out, and easy to understand. Fortunately, by this time you've already done a lot of this thinking while you made your life plan, clarified your business concept, and drew up your marketing plan. Now you can bring all that thinking together in this document. Make sure not to include any proprietary information about your business. For example, you would never learn the recipe for Kentucky Fried Chicken from the restaurant chain's business plan.

EMERSON'S experience

HERE'S A SAMPLE BUSINESS DESCRIPTION FROM MY FIRST BUSINESS:

Quintessence Multimedia is a full-service multimedia production company. Quintessence develops high-quality marketing products for broadcast or business use in the healthcare and pharmaceutical industries. Core business services include marketing consulting, multicultural outreach, video production, interactive design, and educational multimedia development. We provide our clients with cost-effective marketing products that convey their message accurately and in a compelling fashion. The Quintessence slogan is *"We're in the Business of Helping People Communicate Their Ideas."*

Your business description needs to answers the questions:

- What is your product or core business services?
- What is your unique value proposition?
- What is your competitive advantage?
- How will your product or service meet the needs of your customers?
- What are your product-development milestones?

The market analysis

The market analysis starts with a market summary outlining every customer segment. Then it drills down to how much each customer segment is worth to the business in terms of revenue. Then the total market strategy outlines the marketing approach for each target segment.

Generally, you'll have a greater chance of success if you pursue a business in a growing industry. If you are not in a growth industry, you need to understand how long you can keep your business going before the market moves or is saturated. Will you serve an unmet need in the market? Can you resolve the customer's pain? Be exhaustive about your competition and understand how often and under what conditions the customer buys your product or service.

The marketing plan

In Chapter 8, I reviewed the elements of a marketing plan and why it is so critical in the foundation upon which your business is built. It is critical to know who's buying and why they would buy it from you. If you cannot "see" the face of the customer, there is no use in even finishing the business plan.

Are you selling hot dogs and sandwiches on a busy college campus? Your student-customer is clear. Will you specialize in quality shirts for big and tall men? Your customer is now specific and unique. In either case, you will have to give a reason for those customers to purchase from your company. This leads directly to your position in the market. Whether it is to provide "the highest-quality beef hot dogs at the lowest price" or to have "the widest range of sizes in high-quality men's shirts," it becomes the reason why a customer picks you over your competitor. Your marketing plan should convey to anyone reading your business plan what you see as your competitive advantage.

You must explain your basic product offerings or core services. Understand the number and type of potential customers (Gen X, Gen Y, Gen D, Baby Boomers, etc.); pricing; placement, promotion, competition; sales and so much more go into a solid marketing plan.

The operations plan

This explains how you plan to run the business on a day-to-day level. Managing your enterprise is serious work. As the boss, you need to orchestrate how the business will run while keeping costs down and maximizing profits. You need to have a clear process for delivery, handling customer complaints, determining how many employees you need, using discounts, and much more.

If you are manufacturing a product, it is important to establish how you will track all the raw materials, processes, finished goods, and shipped goods, and to know how you will handle the many emergencies, large and small, that will arise. Your business plan should include as much detail as you can so anyone can see how you expect things to work.

Running your business can be as simple as going to a big box retailer and stocking up on more hot dogs, rolls, condiments, napkins, soda, etc. for that week's business of running a hot dog stand. Or it can be as complicated as contracting with a foreign manufacturer to create luxury shirts, getting them through customs, price-tagging them for sale, stocking the store, scheduling help, and much more.

Other issues that fall under operations include location, business permits, inventory management, power and communications needs, insurance requirements, additional construction needs, and zoning requirements. Any of these areas can stop you from opening your doors and should be addressed as a detailed part of your plan. Personnel issues like pay, skills set needed, training, and total headcount should also be touched on as they have a direct impact on your operations plan and your financial projections. See Chapter 17 for more details on this topic.

The management team

Highlighting your expertise and background is critical to giving your business credibility, particularly in the early years. My first business was a multimedia production company, and my background as a television producer was key to persuading my clients to trust me with their marketing projects. Your knowledge of your industry and your relationships with potential strategic partners and customers will be an important asset to your business. As your business grows and your management team takes shape, any new managers should have diverse business experiences, significant business contacts, demonstrated leadership, and/or technical savvy. Your business plan must explain what sort of management team you will put together. (Of course, if you're the only one involved in the business, this issue doesn't apply.)

Intellectual property strategy

Once you develop a concept or a product that you want to introduce into the marketplace, you should consider whether that idea is subject to intellectual property protections. This applies particularly to anyone starting a business that involves creating proprietary computer software, but the definition of intellectual property can be expanded to cover quite a number of other things. You may need to file a patent application or register a copyright to protect your idea. If you are using a special trade name or a symbol associated with your business name, you might need to register your trademark or trade name so that competitors will not be able to use your intellectual property.

Seek the advice of an intellectual property attorney. If you choose to register your intellectual property yourself, you'll need to understand a few basic concepts to determine what kinds of protections are available for your original ideas and concepts.

Trademarks/Trade names. A trademark (™) is a distinctive sign or symbol used by a business to identify to consumers the source of its products and services. A trademark will distinguish your products or services from those of other businesses. A trademark can be a name, word, phrase, symbol, logo, design, image, or a combination of these.

The owner of a registered trademark can bring a lawsuit for trademark infringement to prevent the unauthorized use of that trademark. However, you're not required to register your trademark. The owner of an unregistered trademark may also file suit for infringement, but the trademark can only be protected within the geographical area in which it has been used.

Trade secret. A trade secret is a special formula, process, design, pattern, practice, or compilation of information used by a business to gain a competitive advantage. For example, the secret formula for making Coca-Cola is a protected trade secret. The method you use for doing business, your customer lists, your client files . . . these are trade secrets.

A business owner need not register trade secrets to secure protection. Instead, you need to make sure that your employees understand they are under a duty of confidentiality not to disclose any trade secrets. Consider having them sign a nondisclosure, noncompete agreement when you hire them. Your attorney can draw up this document for you.

Copyrights. The creator of an original work, such as song, a book, a film, or a software package, is entitled to exclusive-use rights under copyright laws. If you have an employee write a computer program to run software on your business systems, you are entitled to copyright protection to keep other businesses from copying your computer software. This will allow you as the business owner to exploit the financial value of any original works prepared by you or your employees. Any original work your employees create while on the clock become the intellectual property of your business.

As the copyright holder, you have the right to copy the work, make adaptations, and sell or license the right to use the copyrighted works to other businesses and individuals. To obtain this protection, the original work need only be fixed in a tangible medium such as a writing, a recording, or saved in a file format. I always advise business owners to obtain a formal copyright registration with the United States Copyright Office in Washington, D.C. It is inexpensive and provides peace of mind and the necessary documentation in case you need to file a copyright infringement suit against a competitor.

EMERSON'S essentials

There is no such thing as the poor man's copyright protection. *Please do not think that you have copyright protection by mailing yourself a copy of your work in a sealed envelope.*

Patents. If you have developed a product that does something no other product does, you need to obtain a patent. This applies to any new and useful process, machine, method, or design. Your patent application will have to describe in some detail claims concerning your invention to show what is unique about it. A good patent lawyer can help you prepare an application and submit it to the United States Patent and Trademark Office.

Intellectual property checklist
Use this checklist to decide whether you need to protect any of your business ideas and products.

❑ Is your product/service unique?
❑ Is your production process unique?
❑ Are you are using a specialized process or formula that could be patented?

To find a reliable intellectual property lawyer, ask for a referral from the lawyer who helped you incorporate your business. Keep in mind investors will want to know if your product or service can be, or is, protected. Good legal advice is valuable beyond measure when it comes to intellectual property. As soon as you can, engage a patent or copyright lawyer who has experience with small business owners.

The financial plan

The financial plan lays out your operational budget and sales expectations for your business. Typically, the first thing any investor or bank will want to know is how much money your business will generate and by when. You will need to create a tight, well-thought-out, realistic financial plan that includes the amount of personal financial risk you are willing to take. If you are not comfortable with accounting, you should engage an accountant or a seasoned bookkeeper to help you pull together your initial financial projections.

EMERSON'S essentials

It is a good idea to work alongside your accountant for a while once you start doing business. *That's the best way to grasp the financial inner workings of your company.*

I was not able to really understand my company's financial statements until I was in business nearly two years. Do not let this happen to you. You need up-to-date financial information to make informed business decisions. Using the spreadsheets included with business plan software and business planning books will make developing the financial plan a lot easier.

Your financial plan is your best estimate of your company's financial future. It is only an estimate because you have no idea how your company will financially perform until you have operated the business for six months to a year. Your plan should include a one-year operating budget and up to three years of company sales projections.

EMERSON'S essentials

When it comes to developing sales projections, be conservative and realistic. *Know your numbers, and be able to defend them. The worst thing you can do is develop financial projections that don't make sense, particularly if you plan to pursue funding.*

Your plan should also include a cash-flow projection and a break-even analysis. The process of developing your financial plan will help you understand how many sales must be generated to cover your expenses and eventually earn the company a profit.

A good financial plan section should include the following information:

EXPENSES

- Projected manufacturing costs (e.g., what it will cost to make your product or provide your service)
- Projected operating expenses (e.g., office rental, supplies, etc.)
- Salaries (including what you will pay yourself and what you will pay your employees)
- Freelance/contract employee expenses (e.g., the cost of retaining a lawyer and an accountant)
- Start-up costs
- Marketing expenses (drawn from the marketing plan)
- Projected business taxes
- Projected revenue, broken down by product line and source

Your financial plan should cover at least one year of operations so you can see how your business will be doing at the end of twelve months. Remember that certain expenses, such as some of your start-up costs, can be amortized over those twelve months.

The Best Way to Write a Business Plan

There are many books available that will help you write your business plan. Many now include spreadsheet templates, which will assist you in developing your initial financial projections. That's a nice feature because developing an operating budget and sales projections are the hardest sections of the plan for most people. The books also include helpful resource guides. I've listed some of the best ones at the back of this book.

You can also hire a consultant to write your business plan. This option may sound attractive, but since you have all the information the consultant will be using, it's more cost-effective to do it yourself. Keep in mind that the cost of hiring a consultant can range from $1,500–$5,000.

You can also purchase business plan software, which costs $75–$200, at any office supply store. In my opinion this is the best option. The software will be up-to-date and will walk you step-by-step through each area of the business plan, including developing your financial projections. Such software also often includes hundreds of business plan templates that you can use to develop your plan. In the back of this book, you'll find some recommendations for some of the more popular business plan software on the market.

Finally, I suggest that you take a business plan course at a local community college, the Small Business Administration, or a Small Business Development Center (SBDC) on how to write a business plan. Fees for such courses can run from $75–$500, but it will be money well spent. For more information on SBA courses, call 1-800-8-ASK-SBA or use this link: *www.sba.gov/aboutsba/sbaprograms/sbdc/sbdclocator/SBDC_LOCATOR.html.*

I have developed a custom business plan template, which you can download at *www.succeedasyourownboss.com.* It also seamlessly integrates into Business Plan Pro software.

Think about your business plan as a living and breathing document that you should review and update every six months to make sure your business is on the right track.

EMERSON'S action steps

[1] Understand the three main uses for a business plan: communication, management, and planning.

[2] Use socio-economic data and industry trends to support your business model.

[3] Use the experience and management skills of the business owner(s) to build the case for why your business will be successful.

[4] Have an intellectual-property protection strategy, and engage an intellectual property attorney to protect your idea or process.

[5] Work with your accountant to develop an operating budget and realistic financial projections.

[6] Download my custom business plan template at *www .succeedasyourownboss.com.*

[7] Purchase business-plan software.

[8] Take a business plan course to complete the plan.

11

GET YOUR FINANCING TOGETHER

$$\left[\textit{ Eight months before you start }\right]$$

Business runs on money. That's a reality you'll have to come to terms with before opening your doors and keep in the front of your thoughts every day you run your business.

To get the business going, you'll need money for your start-up costs. This chapter discusses many options for finding the money to build your entrepreneurial dream. Which option you choose is based on your situation and how much risk you are able and willing to bear. I will discuss the positive and negative factors of each option, including using savings, 401(k) loans, money from friends and family, home equity loans, angel investors, venture capitalists, and bank loans. After considering all these possibilities, you need to decide which financial choice makes the most sense in order to make your dream a reality.

Nobody will buy into your dream if you don't. *You must be willing to invest your own cash in your business; after all, if you don't have the confidence to back your idea, why should anyone else? But please consider all the risks before spending your life savings on your business.*

Savings

Your savings account is one of the best ways to finance your new business venture. If you have followed the advice in Chapter 4, you have spent time trimming your spending habits and accumulating personal funds that you can access to start your business. This is money that is not necessary to meet your everyday living expenses. Keep in mind as well that I am not suggesting you put at risk your emergency funds.

You can, of course, take money directly out of your savings account and spend it on start-up costs. But it's also possible to leave your money in savings or a money market account, letting it continue to earn interest, and instead use your savings as leverage to get the cash you need.

For example, if you purchase CDs—Certificates of Deposits, you can use them as collateral for a loan. You will earn interest on the CD (usually from 2 to 5 percent), which lowers the cost of the loan. Talk about a win/win!

The benefits of this approach are:

■ This is a great way to borrow if you have less than stellar credit, and it keeps your borrowing costs low.

- Because you are borrowing against your own money, there is no need to convince a banker to believe in your plan—you believe in yourself and put your own money behind it.
- It's quick. You can usually leave your old job sooner if you have the financing for your new business in place, allowing you to focus 100 percent of your time on the business.
- By buying brokered CDs you can shop for the best and purchase CDs from banks around the country. CDs are federally insured up to $100,000, so it doesn't matter where you purchase them.

Drawbacks to this approach include:

- If you default on your loan, you risk losing all of your money invested in the CDs.
- Using personal funds as collateral effectively ties up the money, preventing you from using it in other ways.
- Interest rates can change and go higher.

Balancing advantages against drawbacks, this is one of the best ways to borrow money for your business. You will have maximum flexibility and freedom to operate. At the same time, as with all possible methods of raising start-up funds, you must decide how big a risk you're willing to take.

Your Retirement Fund

Now could be the time to borrow against your 401(k) in order to finance your life's dream. Overall this is a great source of borrowing, assuming you are in a position to keep your job during the twelve months prior to starting your business. For that year, you will continue to put money into your account. If your company matches the funds you put into the account, so much the better.

Borrowing against your 401(k) allows you to use your own money and then pay it back to yourself.

EMERSON'S essentials

Pay yourself from your business's profits. *As your business begins to make money, plan to pay back the money you took from your retirement account or savings to fund its start-up. Put that cost in your budget so you stick to it.*

The benefits of this approach include:

- You can usually borrow up to 50 percent of the vested balance of your retirement account or $50,000, whichever is less.
- Assuming you make interest payments on time, you will pay little or no taxes or penalties.
- The interest you are paying is going back into your account, not to the bank.

The drawbacks of borrowing against your retirement account include:

- Most plans have a five-year repayment cycle. If you leave your job before the loan is repaid, it will become due within a short time after you announce that you are leaving your company.
- You can only borrow against your 401(k) if you have your job. If you become a victim of corporate downsizing or leave your job to start the business, you must repay the loan within thirty to ninety days to avoid heavy taxes and penalties.

- There are extra withdrawal penalties if you are less that fifty-nine-and-a-half years of age and cannot repay the loan.
- There can be fees or maintenance charges to borrow the funds. Discuss your 401(k) account with your plan coordinator or your company's human resource representative (although you don't need to tell them that you're planning to use the funds for start-up costs for your business).

In general, you should discuss your plan with your accountant before borrowing any money from your 401(k). If you are over the age of fifty and thus beginning to near the age for retirement, you may not want to use this source to fund your business. It's not a good idea to mortgage your future retirement to start your business when there are other ways of getting seed capital.

Home Equity Line of Credit

This was once the most common way to fund a business. Since the beginning of the downturn in the U.S. housing market in 2007, it has become less popular. All things considered though, this still a great way to fund your business, assuming you have substantial equity in your home.

You should not borrow more than 80 percent of your home's value, and if you go beyond 80 percent, your lender will probably require you to buy private mortgage insurance (PMI).

Having a golden credit score (700 or higher) is your best asset in obtaining a home equity loan and keeping your borrowing costs down. It could allow you the freedom to stretch out the payment schedule from five to twenty years.

A Home Equity Line of Credit (HELOC) generally carries a variable interest rate. Current interest rates and the condition of the borrowing market are the biggest factors in your decision on this type of financing. The markets usually change in waves, but if you have a low interest rate on your first mortgage, keep it and look at HELOC. If you have a high interest rate relative to the current market, first consider refinancing. This will put you in the best borrowing position. The benefits of this approach include:

■ You can access the funds quickly and easily. If you already have an established HELOC, you can just write a check against the line of credit. If you don't, opening a home equity line of credit is a relatively simple procedure.

■ The interest is deductible on your taxes, as it is mortgage interest.

■ There are options to ensure you get the lowest interest rate possible.

Drawbacks include:

■ Using home equity means you are using your house as collateral. Never forget this. If your business fails and you cannot repay the loan, the bank can take actions to foreclose on your home.

■ The overall housing market can affect your ability to get this type of loan.

■ HELOC interest rates are adjustable and may rise higher than other sources.

■ If you borrow more than 80 percent of the value of your home, you will almost certainly have to purchase Private Mortgage Insurance (PMI). This can be a significant added expense, so in general never borrow more than 80 percent of your home's value.

■ A new loan against your home will require an appraisal of the value of your home. This can be a problem if the housing market has been in decline and houses in your area have lost value.

■ If you borrow too much and the house loses value, you could wind up owing more than the house is worth. (This is referred to as "being upside down on your mortgage.")

EMERSON'S essentials

Using home equity means you are borrowing against your home and you could lose your home. *A home equity loan is a good way to fund your dream, but especially in a down housing market, there is a substantial amount of risk. Be careful not to put your home in peril recklessly in pursuit of your dream.*

Friends and Family

This can be the best or worst source of money for starting a business. Family members often can lend you the funding you need, but repayment terms can potentially cause a rift in the family.

Sometimes family members will want a piece of the business in exchange for the loan. Others might believe their loan gives them a license to freely advise you on the best way to run your business. Many times your family members do not understand it typically takes eighteen months for a new business to break even, let alone turn a profit. They might call you every week or month to ask how the business is doing. None of this makes for a happy business owner. But if you need funding and a friend or family member is willing to lend it to you, you may need to suck it up for your dream. You can tolerate anything for a little while.

The positive side of borrowing from friends and family is that they're in the best position to understand your passion for your business. Many successful small businesses have been started with loans from parents, friends, or in-laws.

Your best option is to find a family member who is reasonable to deal with and happy to be a silent partner. Be sure to agree on reasonable borrowing terms. I advise you to always pay some interest to the lender, however small. This will help you skirt the IRS laws on gifts (please see your accountant for more details).

Although you're borrowing from someone you know, perhaps intimately, still document the agreement in writing so everyone is clear on the terms, should any problems arise. Have your attorney draw up a contract that everyone can sign.

Bank Loans

Typically, banks do not give loans to start-up businesses. There are franchises that facilitate and assist with start-up funding, but most often bank loans are only practical if you have been in business for two to three years. You need to show a bank your track record including revenues, cash flow management, budgets, and personal credit profiles. In most cases, you will need to sign a personal guarantee or provide cosigners in order to qualify for a loan. Seek out banks that are more receptive to working with small businesses. Many national banks chains cannot adequately service the needs of very small businesses. These banks will require significant collateral and move faster in terms of processing the loan, but they are much more rigid in their loan requirements. Also, most loan decisions are not made locally, so the person you have the relationship with may have limited or no influence over your loan decision.

Smaller banks can be more flexible, and you will usually be dealing with a local decision maker. (See Chapter 21 for more information on banking relationships.)

To sum up how a bank will examine your application, keep in mind the six Cs:

1. **Capacity**. Your ability to repay the loan. This is the single most important factor your bank will consider in deciding whether to advance you money. Your cash-flow statement in your financial plan will provide the answer. A good cash-flow statement details your ability to repay the loan in a timely manner.

2. **Credit**. What is your personal credit score? Banks will require you to sign a personal guarantee on a loan to share the risk. The higher your credit score, the more favorable terms you can negotiate.

3. **Capital**. How much money you need and how you will use those funds. The more money you ask for, the more scrutiny your loan application will receive. Educate yourself about the types and amounts of loans your bank will typical approve.

4. **Collateral**. The assets you can provide as security for your loan. These could include your house, your car, or your business assets, particularly if you have expensive equipment (trucks, industrial printers, broadcast video cameras, etc.) Collateral greatly increases your chances of getting a loan. Beware, however, of lenders that over-collateralize loans. Watch for phrases in your loans papers like, "We will take a business lien on all current and future business assets." That is a steep price to pay for a $35,000 loan.

5. **Character**. Your reputation. Who knows you? Are you trustworthy? Smaller, local banks will look at this aspect closely. As well, all banks will look at your business experience and your industry background.

6. **Conditions**. Your loan's terms and conditions. Is it a good deal for you or the lender? Your bank wants to make sure that you are using the loan for a legitimate business purpose. Some lenders will require invoices from your vendors and will cut checks directly to the vendors for payment.

EMERSON'S essentials

Be careful not to tie up all your business assets as collateral on a very small loan. *When you grow and need a much bigger loan, you will not have those assets available as collateral. Your first loan, hopefully, will not be your last.*

Do not forget to consider credit unions and nonprofit organizations as potential lending partners. Such organizations typically give smaller loans than banks do, but once you build a track record, you can go after a higher dollar amount with any lending institution.

It's possible that you may not want to borrow the money to cover your start-up costs, either because you have only a fair credit rating or because you have a low tolerance for risk, and borrowing always involves some risk. Now, rather than borrowing the money, let's consider getting outside investors.

Angel Investors

There are many people who have a lot of money. Possibly they've inherited wealth or maybe they're successful entrepreneurs or businesspeople who have cashed out but still yearn for the thrill of business ownership without the daily grind. Such people have a lot of discretionary income and are willing to help others who have ideas and energy. Angel investors are interested in making money, but they do not need or want daily interaction with the business.

Unlike venture capitalists (see below), such investors don't typically demand management control, financial control, or payback within five years. Angels will often serve as senior advisors or board members for your business, but they rarely want to be involved in the direct management of the company.

Angel investors usually will fund lower-growth-rate projects or smaller business ideas than venture capitalists. They are also more tolerant of high-risk businesses than are venture capitalists. For some it is not just about the money—they want to give back. Many of them thrive on the energy new entrepreneurs radiate.

An investor is different from a lender. Angel investors will generally become your business partners, and in return for their investment capital, they will want a substantial amount of equity in the business.

EMERSON'S essentials

Angel investment can make your business soar—but only if your idea is strong. *One of the most famous cases of an angel investor was when Sun Microsystems founder Andy Bechtolsheim wrote out a check for $100,000 to Larry Page and Sergey Brin to start a business manufacturing and selling search-engine software. Page and Brin decided to call their company Google. And we know how that ended up!*

Finding an angel is not a quick process. Often it can take up to three years to secure angel funding. Angels are looking for talent first and great ideas second. And they can come from lots of different places:

- **Friends and family**. Your uncle or aunt or next-door neighbor may not be willing to lend you money to start your business. They might, however, want to invest in it, if they believe in you and your idea.
- **Local retired businesspeople**. Often wealthy retirees want to give something back to their community. If you are starting a local business that will clearly benefit your neighborhood, you may seem like a good investment opportunity.
- **Organizations**. Sometimes angels gather in groups so they can pool their resources and expand their funding. For example, in my area a prominent angel group is Robin Hood Ventures, located in Philadelphia, who "have joined together to fund and aid the development of local companies through their collective business experience and contacts."

Your success in reaching angel investors and convincing them to back your business will heavily depend on your skills delivering your pitch for your business (also known as a "thirty-second commercial" or your "elevator pitch"). Angels want business owners who are working hard to develop their ideas, can articulate their product, vision, and target market, and have the management skills to lead a successful business.

EMERSON'S essentials

You must have a strong elevator pitch about your business. *Practice this in front of a mirror, to your spouse, to your friends, or to anyone else who will listen. Pare it down so you've got the essentials of your business in a strong, compelling, and brief presentation. You should be able to deliver this pitch in thirty-seconds at most.*

Venture Capitalists (VCs) or Private Equity Investors

Venture capitalists (VCs) are looking for business ventures that will grow fast and be bought by other, larger companies at a significant profit to stockholders, or that will let investors cash out in three to five years at a significant rate of return (typically 30 percent to 100 percent). Venture capitalist firms, also known as private equity firms, typically manage their investments like stock portfolios or pension funds, betting that a few investments will hit it big in order to fund all of the ones that do not make it. They are not passive investors and will want to see a detailed business plan with financial projections with an eye toward accelerated growth.

Lining up venture capital is not a quick process and can take even longer than getting backing from an angel investor. It can take up to three years to secure venture funding.

VCs will typically take a controlling stake (meaning controlling ownership) in the firm, hold financial control of the business (meaning check-writing authority), and eventually will bring in their own management team to ensure that the business is run in a manner consistent with their growth objectives. Sensitive entrepreneurs, beware. If you're used to calling all the shots, VCs can be pushy and hard to work with. They monitor business progress regularly, and demand that management make decisions in the investors' best interests.

An investment agreement drawn up by venture capitalists will include milestones you must reach, usually measured by financial metrics such as revenue growth, profitability, etc. If you fail to meet these milestones, the VCs will gain increased control of the business.

The good thing about venture capitalists is that they have the money and the management experience that many small business owners lack. They also have insight and access to connections that could make the difference between being a huge success and losing everything. In my opinion, this is the most expensive capital in the marketplace, but in some cases is it the only viable option. VCs are not the easiest way to finance your business, but if they like your idea, that means they think you could become the next Yahoo, Google, or Microsoft. For a directory of venture capital firms and angel investors, check out *www.vfinance.com*.

EMERSON'S experience

Here's a VC story for you. My friend, Sam, created a dot.com company in the financial sector. Years earlier and straight out of business school, he had worked on the management team of a successful dot.com that went public. During his time with that company, Sam identified an unmet niche in the marketplace. He pulled his money together, secured a few small investors, and struck out on his own to create his dot.com venture. In the first few years he had revenues over $2 million, but he knew that he needed VC money to meaningfully grow his business.

Sam hit the angel and venture capital circuit. He signed up for every venture capital fair he could travel to. He mastered the perfect pitch. Eventually, he fixed his sights on a celebrity venture capitalist. Every time I saw him, he said, "If I could just meet that guy, I believe I could convince him to invest in my business."

After a year on the hunt, he finally got an audience with this celebrity VC. The man was so impressed that not only did he invest in Sam's business, he became the company's largest shareholder and chairman of the board of directors. With the infusion of new capital, the company added more professional staff and grew significantly.

A little more than two years later, the company issued a press release announcing that Sam would be stepping down as CEO of his company. The press release said that the board would immediately commission a search for a chief executive who had demonstrated experience in managing the successful growth of financial services companies.

The lesson is clear: When you invite venture capital in, it is not exactly your company anymore. Every day you must prove to them that you have the skills and vision to remain in the big chair.

EMERSON'S action steps

[1] Determine the amount of money you will need to start up your business; then draw up a list of possible sources for the money.

[2] Evaluate the amount of risk you are willing to take. This will go a long way in deciding how you want to raise your start-up capital.

[3] If you are considering borrowing against your 401(k) account, remember that you must hold onto your current job until the loan is paid off.

[4] Make a list of local angel investors who might be interested in your business idea, including angel investor consortiums in your locality.

[5] Compile a list of possible venture capitalists and find out if there are any VC fairs taking place in your area.

[6] Prepare a thirty-second pitch for your business idea.

12

BRAND YOUR BUSINESS

$$\left[\ \textit{Seven months before you start}\ \right]$$

Now you've got a business plan in place and you know where the money is coming from to start up your business and keep it running for the first twelve months. It's time to move on to the next project: branding. After doing thorough market research and checking out the competition, you must start developing a brand identity.

Defining a Brand

What is a brand? It is the image or culture you create for your product or service. It is also your business name and how that name is visually expressed. A logo is part of it, but a brand is much more. Essentially, a brand is how you want people to perceive your business.

When building a brand, credibility counts. And like everything else you do in business, building a credible brand requires knowing your target audience. It's a slow process, since it takes time to win your customers' trust and time to communicate clearly to them the character of your business. But for all the time you'll put into it, branding is one of the most important things you'll do. Branding is about getting your key audience to see you as the only one that provides a solution to their problem.

EMERSON'S essentials

Branding doesn't stop when your business starts. *Building your brand is something you'll do for as long as you operate your business. You may even, during the course of your business, change your brand several times. Harley-Davidson, for example, successfully rebranded itself from its outlaw biker image to a company that makes expensive toys for middle-aged guys.*

You brand a name and market a product. Think of branding as living with consistent values and marketing as taking one good shot at sales. Your brand must be expressed throughout your business, both in the way you market your product and in the appearance of your company materials. Your business cards, letterhead, envelopes, folders, signage, and other corporate branding materials should all have a consistent logo, business colors, and tag line. Ask your graphic designer for your exact PMS or Pantone colors and a font style guide so that you can always keep your colors and fonts consistent.

When it comes to developing your brand identity, there are two schools of thought. You can hire a firm to help you name and brand yourself, or you can pull together your kitchen cabinet of advisors and a few close friends willing to work for food and have a good old brainstorming session.

Your logo

Why do you need a logo? Erin Ferree, a marketing design strategist and owner of elf design, says, "Forty percent of people better remember what they see over what they hear or read. So having graphics associated with your business will make you more memorable in the mind of a potential client." A well-designed logo gives you a major edge in a competitive marketplace.

Once you name your business, hire a professional graphic designer to develop your logo. Do not, use clip art, free art on the web or stylized fonts as your logo. This is not only unprofessional, but it immediately screams "newbie small business owner."

The benefits of a professionally designed logo are numerous. It can permit you to:

Look more established. A professional-looking logo says that your company is going to be around for a while and should be taken seriously. It will be a big help in winning the immediate respect of clients and vendors.

Attract clients. A strong logo on your marketing materials can help you to meet prospective clients. Corporations are filled with gatekeepers whose job it is to screen small business representatives. No one will risk his or her reputation on a small business that doesn't present itself well in all aspects of its business.

Convey trustworthiness. A colorful, distinctive logo, professional collateral material, and up-to-date website shows that you are a serious about your business and committed to your clients.

Explain an unusual line of business. In a highly technical or offbeat industry, a professional logo can visually clarify what you do.

Explain your company name. If your company name contains a fictitious word, jargon, or an acronym, the logo can help explain its meaning. With compelling graphics, potential clients are more likely to remember you.

EMERSON'S experience

The name of my first business was Quintessence Multimedia. "Quintessence" is a noun that means perfection. I chose it because it was a nice-sounding word with a powerful meaning. I picked it up from a friend when I was a sophomore in college. She had a perfect 4.0 grade average in biochemistry, and her sorority sisters called her "Quintessence."

When it came time to design the logo for Quintessence Multimedia, my graphic designer and I decided that I needed to emphasize the Q in the logo and use PMS 200 red and black as my main brand colors. My business cards are red, and I always stand out in a crowd. To this day, even when people cannot remember my name, they say, "Oh, that's Ms. Quintessence."

Collateral materials

Your logo should appear on all your collateral materials. These should include at least:

- Website
- Stationery

- Envelopes
- Packing labels
- Business cards

Business cards are especially important; when you're networking, you'll hand them out extensively. You must rely on your business card to make a good impression on a potential client or vendor long after you're gone.

EMERSON'S essentials

Avoid those free business cards that online printing services offer. *They look generic and unprofessional. New businesses crop up every week, and your company may not last if it lacks a well-defined brand. Differentiation is key.*

I went to a networking function a few years ago. There must have been 300 small business owners in attendance. I am a pretty aggressive networker, and I probably talked with forty to fifty people that night. When I got to my office the next morning, I went through my purse to review the business cards of all the people I had met. Four of them had the exact same free business-card design. The back of the card even said the business cards were free. I was immediately turned off, and none of the people were memorable. I tossed their cards in the trash because I did not take them seriously.

Be sure to use your brand's colors on all your materials. The more you associate your logo and colors with your company, the more people will naturally make the leap and think of you when they see them.

Marketing Collateral

As you start your business, you will need to provide information about your company's products and services to anyone who could possibly help you. Your ability to get a foot in the door depends in part upon how well you tell your company's story. It will be important to highlight solutions you deliver for your clients. Every small business owner should always have marketing collateral on hand, ready to distribute it to perspective customers (in hard copy and electronic versions).

Write a mission and philosophy statement

Write four to five paragraphs about the heart and soul of your business. You will use this copy in e-mails and proposals. The document should include a description of the core services you provide, the types of projects you specialize in, and the unique value you bring to the market. It should also explain where you're located, who works for you, what specialized equipment you use, and a short company history. Don't forget as well to include contact information on this and every piece of marketing collateral: either a full address and phone number or at least an e-mail address.

Company fact sheet

Your company fact sheet can be one-sided or two-sided and should explain what you do, what customers you serve, and what problems you solve. It should also include the following information:

- Your company name and logo
- Brief company biography and slogan
- Description and photos of products or services
- Brief customer list
- Certifications

- Location of headquarters and any affiliate offices
- Contact information

Case studies/product fact sheet

If you are a service business, you can't talk about a tangible product. Instead, develop case studies for high-profile and marquee projects your company has been involved in. This information can be used on your company's website. Try to include a few testimonials from satisfied clients, if possible. Case studies and product fact sheets should include the following:

- Type of service category
- Name of client
- Purpose of the project (e.g., to raise awareness, to build sales, to increase online traffic)
- Execution brief—describe all services provided in more detail
- Outcome for the clients
- Client endorsements of the company

Personnel

Where possible, it's nice to provide a biography of your top company officers. It makes the business seem more human if clients can put a face with a name. Every business owner and all top management should have two biographies. The short one should be roughly 100–250 words; the long biography should be no more than a page and highlight the following:

- Prior jobs/relevant experience
- Client list
- Educational background
- Volunteer community service
- Awards or honors

EMERSON'S experience

Sometimes it is your community service that speaks for you. Participating on boards or in nonprofit organizations can genuinely benefit your business. It's a good way to create a hobby and to build long-lasting relationships.

I once pitched the head of the public relations division of a major Madison Avenue ad agency. It was a cold call; I did not know the woman to whom I was speaking. I e-mailed her my bio and my company fact sheet when I requested the meeting. All I wanted was twenty minutes of her time.

After several e-mails back and forth, and a good bit of persistence on my part, I did get the meeting, and Quintessence Multimedia got a small piece of business. Years later, I asked her why she granted me the meeting. She said that she noticed in my bio that I had coached a nine- to-ten-year-old girls softball team, and she played softball as a kid.

If you are new to creating your own business, mention your experience in and knowledge of the industry. Later, when you've launched your company, you can create a list of current and former customers. Be careful not to use a customer's trademarked logo on your collateral materials without permission.

Media Kit

Compile a media kit to send to your local business journal and any trade publications when you launch your business, bring a new product to market, or win any business awards. Media kits are also handy to pitch your business at trade shows. They're a further way of reinforcing your brand.

EMERSON'S essentials

Media people are not interested in giving you free publicity. *They want to tell great business stories. Think of a unique angle before you contact media. Make sure you have an answer to the question, "Why would anyone care?"*

Your media kit should include:

A folder with your company's logo on it. You don't need a fancy embossed logo on the folder. That is expensive, and at this point, conserving costs is important to you. Have a graphic designer make you a high-gloss sticker. On a nice folder in one of your brand colors, it will look professional and will not break the bank.

A letter pitching your company. Personalize the pitch letter to your media target. Make it sound as if you're writing specifically to the recipient of the mailing. If asked, send another copy when you call to follow up. Also try pitching to the local and weekend public affairs TV shows, particularly if your product is visually appealing and unique.

A company fact sheet or product fact sheet and a biography of the owner. Make sure you have a story to tell. This is what the media wants. Sample headlines for your pitches might be: Amazing Growth in One Year; Mom Makes Hobby into Big Business; Green Business Makes Greenbacks; SBA Honors Local Small Business.

Articles written about your company. Professional reprints can be costly, but they make a slick presentation. You also can just make the copies yourself. Word to the wise: if the article was done in color, make color copies. Highlighting your media exposure will provide instant credibility. Sometimes reporters want to see that someone else liked you, too.

Your business card. As I've said before, this is essential. Make sure it clearly states your name, title, basic contact information, your website, and your cell phone number in addition to your office phone number. It's also becoming more common to include all your social media contact information. You want to be as accessible as possible.

SAMPLE SOCIAL MEDIA CONTACT LIST

Here's the list of my social media contact information that I include in all my media kits. It may seem a bit like overkill, but the fact of the matter is that, in this business of brand building, too much is better than too little.

Website: *www.melindaemerson.com*
Blog: *www.succeedasyourownboss.com*
Twitter: *http://twitter.com/smallbizlady*
LinkedIn: *www.linkedin.com/in/melindaemerson*
Facebook Fan page: *www.facebook.com/smallbizlady*
Smallbizchat FB group: *http://facebook.com/smallbizchat*
Facebook: *http://facebook.com/melinda.emerson*
YouTube: *www.youtube.com/melindaemerson*

You should have two media kits with you at all times (one in the car and one in your briefcase). Be careful to review and regularly update them. You don't want to distribute dated material. Have a graphic designer create a background and stationery template in MS Word and MS PowerPoint so you can make adjustments to your company fact sheet and product fact sheets quickly, as needed.

Remember at all times that your brand is your reputation. It speaks for you when you do not have a chance to speak for yourself.

EMERSON'S action steps

[1] Determine the kind of image you want your products and services and your company to project to your customers. That's your brand statement.

[2] Hire a graphics professional to develop a logo that reflects your brand. Use the logo and at least two colors in your collateral materials.

[3] Write a four- to five-paragraph company mission explaining what your company will do for its customers.

[4] Develop the basic marketing collateral materials, electronically and in hard copy, as needed. Produce a media kit, and carry two copies at all times

13

SET UP YOUR
ONLINE STRATEGY

$$\left[\textit{ Seven months before you start } \right]$$

In the last chapter, we discussed how your brand and logo are critical to the success of your small business. Your web presence is at least as important. We are now in the digital age. It used to be that all you had to worry about was having a website; now you need a blog and a social media footprint to go along with it. Now people go online to make connections and be entertained. They also go online to do product research, shop, stay informed, and inform others.

Your involvement in this rich environment starts with building your business website.

Designing Your Website Strategy

When it comes to designing a website, you have three options: You can build a traditional website; you can build a traditional website with a blog incorporated; or you can create a blog and use it as your website. There are strong arguments for any of these options, depending on what kind of business you run. I have both a website and a blogsite, an information marketing tactic that works for me.

Let's define the basic business website terms:

A website is a collection of related web pages, images, videos, or other digital assets that are available under a specific domain name on the web. Websites are essentially online brochures designed to do four possible things: provide information, build a contact list, make money, and raise awareness of a small business. A typical website includes five to seven pages: home page, about us, contact us, services/products, in the news, and an online store.

A blog is an online journal written by one person, or a team of staff people, focused on a particular area of interest. Professional blogs are typically written in a conversational style and updated two or three times a week. Since you're starting a new business, it's best to have the blog as part of your website. No matter what method you decide to go with, it is very important to have a static home page on the website and/or blog where your offering is clear the moment someone lands on your page.

Regardless of what option you choose, there are six things you need to address in your website design:

1. **Your market position**. Are you going to be known for selection and delivery? If so, your website must be fast and have a great selection. Your web design, in other words, must reflect the qualities you want your customers to associate with your business.
2. **Your degree of customization**. Are you providing online customized solutions or products for customers based on information collected from surveys and registration data? Your site should allow you to highlight benefits that can only be provided efficiently online. Let's say you target pet owners. You can create

a website all about dogs or a website that specializes in beagles. Your site can take visitors through a personalized analysis based on their specific dog.

3. **Your architecture**. Presentation is everything. The architectural design of the website will convey the credibility of the site. Having a website design that looks bad will give the impression that the company is not technologically advanced or isn't willing to invest in its appearance. It's like wearing a badly made suit to a business meeting; you may know what you're talking about, but your first impression will be a poor one. Visitors to a poorly designed site may question the quality of service your company can provide.

4. **Your navigation**. Good websites are easy to use. No one likes a website where you need to search for how to place an order, how to contact company representatives, or how to pay. The links between your pages should be easy to use, fast, and direct. Experiment with how many clicks it takes to get from the opening page of the site to placing an order. The fewer the better.

5. **Your expertise**. The quality and quantity of content on the site are important in demonstrating the company's expertise. This is an opportunity for you to explain what makes your products and services different from your competitors. Your website should indicate who you are, what services or products you offer, your industry focus, and your contact information. Use keywords to help your content show up in search engines. Consider having helpful links on your website to third-party sites that provide more industry information. If your blog is a separate URL, be sure to link your main site to it.

6. **Your trustworthiness**. Every website and blog wants to be perceived as "trustworthy." Make sure your site includes a street address for your company. Having just a phone number and a post office box may lead visitors to question the legitimacy and

quality of your business. Include the name of a contact person on the site. Visitors want to know there's a real person they can call if they need to return a product.

Building Your Website

When it comes time to build a website for your business there are some steps that will maximize your success once you go live.

Secure a web domain name

A good domain name is one that is memorable or that relates to something visitors are interested in. If you can include a keyword in your web address, all the better for search engine optimization (SEO). My suggestion is that you purchase at least two versions of your web domain name (.com, .net or .info). There are many companies available online that you can use to register a domain name. Among the largest are:

- Go Daddy: *www.godaddy.com*
- Dotster: *www.dotster.com*
- Register.com: *www.register.com*
- Moniker Online Services: *www.moniker.com*

Don't ask your web designer to register the name for you; do it yourself. Too many people have had trouble getting their name away from a designer during a dispute.

Purchasing a domain name will cost you between $10 and $35. Paying this fee entitles you to use the name for a year or more with the option at the end of that time to reregister it. Selection and purchase can be a time-consuming process only because so many domain names have already been taken.

Select a professional web hosting company

A web hosting company provides server space for your website. The space includes all your e-mail addresses, web pages, graphics, files, databases, etc. A typical website uses 20–30 MB. You want to make sure that you have enough space not only to build your current website, but to expand in the future as your company grows. Also, make sure your web host provides a statistics package, so that you can track your site's unique visitors. You also need to ask if they can accommodate blogs and online shopping carts.

When selecting your web-hosting provider, ask these questions:

- How many customers do they serve?
- How secure is the site? What type of protection do they offer?
- How much storage do they provide? (100 MB is a good starting point.)
- Will my hosting package also support a blog?
- What are the set-up and monthly fees?
- How many e-mail aliases come with their package?
- How is their technical support and when are they available?

Check out the competition online

You need to know who is out there in the global marketplace. Look at the features and functionality of your competition's websites. Take note of what you like and don't like. If you plan on selling your products online, make sure to examine as many online stores as you can. Take note of the layout and functionality of the online stores and who the vendor is for the shopping cart. I also recommend using *www.alexa.com* as a tool to look at the traffic of your competitors' websites.

Develop a website architecture

You need to think through how you want your website to look and function. One of the simplest ways to develop a website architecture is to use a PowerPoint slide template for an organizational chart. Start with the home page at the top and list the other pages underneath.

Develop a list of keywords and phrases

Before you start developing the content of your site, you need to develop a list of words and phrases people might use to find your business with a search engine. How would someone try to find you? As a rule, you should use the plural of any keywords you want to use, e.g., "dogs" instead of "dog." There are several free and low-cost tools to find which words people are actually using to search the Internet. Try these options:

WordSpot: *www.wordspot.com*
Google: *www.google.com/sktool/#*
Wordtracker: *www.wordtracker.com*

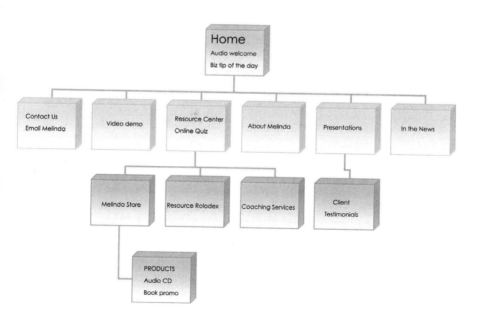

Developing the Content for Your Site

No matter who you hire to build your website, not much can be done until you've created some content for the web pages. This content must, as always, have your customers in mind. After all, they're the ones who'll be reading the pages you put up.

You might consider any of the following:

- Testimonials for your products or services from other industry figures
- Suggestions for how best to use what your company produces
- Information on stores carrying your products

Some material you can include immediately:
- Your mission statement
- A list of products and/or services available
- Information on your company and its officers
- Contact information

A rule of thumb is to put no more than 200 words on a web page. After looking at the competition sites, draft the initial content for your website. Make sure you have someone copyedit it for typos and grammar. Nothing is more unprofessional than typos on your site.

EMERSON'S essentials

Do not expect your web developer to catch any misspellings. *I have found with graphics artists and web developers, the better the artwork, the worse the spelling.*

Hire a professional

Unless you've had experience developing websites, leave it to someone with expertise. Often this is someone you already know—possibly a friend or relative. No matter how well you know the person, do yourself a favor—draw up a formal contract proposal, develop a strict timeline, and use a work-for-hire contract that clearly says you own the finished website. Make sure your vendor has experience designing a website with keyword optimization. Fancy Flash sites are nice, but search engines can't read Flash.

EMERSON'S experience

When I first developed my original website, I hired some friends to develop *www.melindaemerson.com*. I let them register the site domain for me as well as create the artwork and functionality. I knew these people extremely well, and had no concerns about their work or professionalism.

Rather than draw up a contract, we made a verbal agreement, and I paid them all the money for the site before they even began work. It was a big mistake!

I nearly went to court over my website, after they claimed ownership of my domain name. I was dissatisfied with the site they built and wanted to move on to another vendor, and they refused to release the passwords to my site. Luckily, I had filed a trademark for my name and site slogan. My lawyer was able to negotiate control of my site, but only after a lot of trouble and cost. You will find, that, in business, there are plenty of opportunities to learn lessons. Some are more expensive than others.

Create a request for proposal (RFP)

If you don't know anyone who could create your website (and quite possibly, even if you do), you'll need to create a Request for Proposal for a vendor. Make sure to include how much you've budgeted for your site in the request.

Make it clear to your vendor that you want to be able to add pages and make text changes yourself. Get at least three quotes. Good places to find web vendors are Craig's list, *www.elance.com*, and your social media connections; ask other business owners for referrals.

Your vendor should have a portfolio site to review. Require at least three references and call them. Attach your architecture (layout) to the RFP so your potential vendor is clear on how much work is involved.

Buy web authoring software and learn the basics

Do your homework and find out what kind of web development software can work best for your business model. Find out if it comes with a tutorial CD or if one is available. You can use basic software, such as FrontPage or Dreamweaver, but you may find that you need a content management system (CMS). A content management system is a software system used to manage and control a dynamic collection of website material. It also enables you to make changes to your website yourself rather than pay a webmaster to make changes for you.

You must learn some basic things: how to add a page, change text, add graphics and photos, and add a hyperlink. You also need to understand the administration of your site and what your hosting package provides. You need to know your pass codes to access the site and how to add and change e-mail settings. It is best to start learning this stuff as your site is being built, so you can ask your web developer technical questions. You also can take a web development class at a community college to learn some basics.

Select a merchant service account provider

If you want to sell your products or services directly from your website, you'll need a separate merchant service account even if you have an account to take credit cards in your bricks-and-mortar retail store. A Paypal account is a viable option, but it's not the only one. Do your homework and find a credible online credit card vendor. Shop around for the best rates. You can expect a monthly fee and a charge per transaction. Be sure you get the history of the vendor company.

Make sure your merchant service account provider is registered with the Better Business Bureau (BBB). Check to make sure the BBB does not have any open complaints against the company and that you are only paying fees when someone pays you. Some of the credit card companies will try to charge you a monthly fee just to accept their card.

Select a shopping cart system

Your shopping cart system works in tandem with your merchant service account. The right shopping cart makes it easy for people to buy from you. After all, you want to make it as easy as possible for customers to give you their money and receive their merchandise.

Like everything else on the web, a shopping cart system is just software. Once the customer hits the submit button in your store, back-end mechanisms kick into gear to send funds to your account (minus the credit card fees). The shopping cart will send out an e-mail confirmation automatically to the buyer and one to you that signals you or your fulfillment house to mail the customer their merchandise. I use 1ShoppingCart (*www.1shoppingcart.com*) for my online shopping cart system, but there are a number of others available.

Make sure to include your website address on all your marketing and sales material so your customers know where to find you. On your site highlight your niche focus, and use your web presence to establish yourself as an expert in your industry. Update your content often, and focus on creating value for your visitors.

EMERSON'S action steps

[1] Know your target customer and make a list of your keywords before you develop any content for your website.

[2] Hire a professional to build your website.

[3] Thoroughly research web hosting, merchant service accounts, and online shopping carts before deciding on vendors.

[4] Update your content regularly. Search engines love websites with updated content.

14

BUILD YOUR
ONLINE MARKETING

$$\left[\textit{Seven months before you start} \right]$$

Your website is the first step in the critical task of building an online presence for your business. Such a presence is crucial, whether you knit purses, sell tires, teach sales training, provide graphic design services, or have a restaurant. Effective online marketing is about engaging customers where they are online, in the right way at the right time, and most importantly, delivering on your brand promise.

Thanks to online culture, businesses no longer totally control their brands. This might alarm you, but it's actually a good thing for small businesses. Many large corporations in the United States are just starting to figure out the importance of social media, so they do not have a head start on your business. The Internet is a great equalizer.

As long as you are positioned as a problem solver or an expert, many customers will focus on how fast you can provide them with a solution and not how big you are. Because of the amount of data we can now access about our target markets, things like messaging, product demos, and pricing can be customized.

Some may think that going online is confined to young people, but that is not the case. According to the Pew Internet and American Life Project, 79 percent of all adults use the Internet. The number of adults using social networking sites has more than quadrupled, from 8 percent in 2005 to 35 percent in 2008. Nearly one in five adults say they visit blogs, online communities, or social networking sites daily. No matter the age, gender, education, or income level of your target market, a growing number of your customers are using the Internet, and that number will continue to increase.

Building Online Marketing

Social media networking sites give you a chance to meet your customers online. Social media facilitates richer, more meaningful customer connections. When done well, your consumers themselves will promote your products and services.

The face of social media marketing is changing constantly. Current top social media sites include LinkedIn, Facebook, Twitter, and YouTube. But there are hundreds of other options in the social media landscape. There are many free tutorials on the Internet about how to use them. You can also hire a tech-savvy virtual assistant or a social media strategist to teach you what you need to know to get started fast.

EMERSON'S essentials

Give to get. *When you first enter a social media networking site, limit how much you talk about your business. Instead, provide helpful suggestions to others on the site. Add value to the conversations, and you will draw potential clients to you.*

EMERSON'S experience

For years I have been a professional speaker on small business development and have used *www.melindaemerson.com*, LinkedIn, and YouTube to promote my coaching and speaking business. A while ago I starting building an online platform as a small business expert using social media networking sites. My Twitter name is @smallbizlady. For six months, I got on Twitter four times a day, tweeting helpful information about how to run a successful small business and making connections. At the same time, I created a Facebook page.

In early 2009, I started #SmallBizChat, a weekly Twitterchat that works like a talk show except it's done in writing on Twitter. The target for the twitterchat is emerging entrepreneurs who are looking for answers to their start-up business questions. Because #SmallBizChat became so popular, I started, by request, a #SmallBizChat Facebook group for my loyal audience. After I got the hang of Twitter and Facebook, I launched my blog *www.succeedasyourownboss.com*.

My strategy has been to use one social media platform to build another. As I develop new content for my blog, I tweet about it to successfully draw traffic to the website. I also feed my blog content into my LinkedIn and Facebook accounts. I also add value on LinkedIn by asking and answering helpful questions and starting discussions within my numerous LinkedIn groups.

There are few things to keep in mind about social media:

- If you know the online trends of your niche target market, you can rank the social networking sites in order of importance to determine where best to spend your valuable time.
- Develop online profiles right away, just to secure your personal name or business name. Think keywords too.
- Information is not private in social media, so do not badmouth customers or competitors or say anything you wouldn't want your mother to read.
- Be smart about whom you add to your network—quality counts, not quantity. It doesn't matter that you have 30,000 followers on Twitter if you can't influence them to do anything.
- Effective use of social media can lead to viral marketing of your product or service. "Buzz" creates greater awareness of a company, product, or service which in turn generates website visitors or list subscribers that you can turn into sales.
- Getting the endorsement of a high-profile Twitter user, blogger, or reviewer is more helpful in spreading the word about your company and lending it online credibility.

Blogging for Business

A blog can be written by one person, or you can create a company blog, which can be multiauthored. Blogs usually focus on a specific topic; for example, I blog about small business development from a start-up perspective.

Getting your blog noticed on the web isn't easy. It takes a lot of work, time, and consistency. But if you're willing to invest those things, a blog can help you become a thought leader in your industry.

Updating your blog content is easy; you don't need any special technical expertise. Blogs are very low cost, even if you want to customize yours. The cost to build a custom blog URL is $200–$400 for set-up, and the maintenance will run about $150 a year.

Subscribe to a few blogs to get a feel for what blogging sounds like. Your company blog will not work if it just spouts company information. Your content needs to contain useful information that your target market wants.

Here are the essential steps to creating a successful blog:

Define your target customer. Look at their main characteristics (age, education, income, etc.) and find out where they hang out online. You should have already done this back in chapters 8 and 9.

EMERSON'S essentials

Don't use any social media networking sites or develop any blog content until you know exactly whom you are trying to attract as a customer. *Learn the culture of each site you plan to use.*

Create unique content. Make a list of the topics you want to cover in your first 50–100 blog posts, and start writing them. Typical blog posts are between 500–800 words. Since it's seven months before you open your business, if you get started right now, you'll have content that will keep you going for a while once your business opens its doors.

Collect trade publications and other news articles about your industry. They will give you ideas for blog posts and experts you can quote. One of the best things you can do for your blog is highlight other people's expertise.

Building Your Blog

You can either incorporate your blog into your company's website or you can establish it as a stand-alone website. Check out sites such as *www.livejournal.com* for practical information on how to create the blog. You'll need the following material:

> **Your front-page blurb**—As soon as someone clicks on your blog link, they need to know what your blog is about. Tell people what you can do for them and include keywords, your name, and your book name, if you have one. Be sure to balance keywords and expertise.
> **About me**—Include your credentials so your readers can see why they should take seriously what you say.
> **A "blog roll"**—This is a series of links to useful blogs/resources.
> **Services page**—This explains how to hire you.
> **Contact info**—Do not just list your address, phone, and e-mail. Provide links that connect with all your social media accounts as well.

Things to keep in mind

When you are ready to launch your blog, you'll also be ready to launch your business. If you've followed my advice, you'll already have a good deal of content ready to roll. But always include material that's as up-to-date as possible. Reread your entries carefully before posting them.

You can set up your blog so that your blog post titles become the page titles. The page title is the most important thing that search engines look at to determine if your article/post/page should be pulled out of the thousands of possible pages and selected as a search result.

The same words you use in the title also need to appear some-where in your text as well. Just as you did with your web page, look for keywords—words and phrases that an individual will type into a search engine to find your information. Remember, there are a lot of competing blogs out there.

You can use your social media sites to promote your blog content. You can repurpose your blog content in e-newsletters and through article marketing sites. Be sure to make some changes to the content before re-posting it, as search engines do not like duplicate content.

Building an E-Mail List

The most valuable asset to any business is its customers. You must nurture your relationships with your customers by contacting them regularly. E-mail marketing is a cost-effective tool to not only gain new customers but also to retain current ones. The best way to build a list is to provide an incentive to subscribe. Provide something your customers want in exchange for their e-mail address. You can offer incentives in any of the following ways:

E-newsletters. If you provide good information, poten-tial customers will sign up for your e-mail newsletter. It must be relevant and compelling. It may include special promotions or reasons to buy from your business, but it had better include information of interest to your readers. As it is a sales tool, the newsletter should always close with a call to action for the customer, but don't overdo it. Remember, you can repurpose material from your blog to include in your e-newsletter.

Blogs. There should be an opportunity to sign up for your blog on your website and/or blog. You can use an e-mail list or a RSS feed to enroll subscribers.

Free giveaways. Many entrepreneurs develop valuable free materials, products, or services to give away. These are incentives for customers to stay in touch with the company's website and recommend it to their friends. Giveaways can include product samples, special reports, e-books, webinars, and free coaching. People must input their e-mail addresses in order to access the information. On my website, I offer an online quiz, e-newsletter sign-ups, and *12 Cardinal Sins of Small Business and How to Avoid Them!*

EMERSON'S essentials

You should *never* give away something free that is not of high value. *Giving away products and information free is the beginning of a relationship with a potential customer. Do not anger a customer by giving her junk.*

Growing an E-Mail List

To build an e-mail list of your customer base, think about every place that you interact with your customers.

- Do you have a sign-up sheet in your retail location for your mailing list?
- Can you hold a drawing for a prize and ask for participants' e-mail addresses?
- On your website, do you have a link so that people can sign up to receive your company newsletter?
- When you take an order over the phone, do you ask the customer for an e-mail address to send their receipt or shipping confirmation?

How to interact with your list

With e-mail marketing, you can tailor your message to a particular group of your customers. Lisa D. Sparks of Constant Contact says, "It is best to let your personality shine through in your e-mail communications." It's not always just about business. People want to connect directly with you. I make reference to my young son in my social media interactions occasionally, and I find people relate to me more that way. It may also make sense to develop an editorial calendar for your e-mail marketing campaign. For example, if you do a monthly e-newsletter, consider writing all twelve e-newsletters at one time.

Managing your list

Many business owners use customer relationship management (CRM) software to automate their e-mail marketing efforts. Many of these CRM software companies also provide easy-to-use online tools and helpful templates for developing e-mail marketing campaigns. Most also provide tracking data that tell you how many e-mails were opened, by whom, which links were clicked on the most, whether anyone forwarded the message, and whether anyone opted out. This data is helpful to measure the effectiveness of your marketing campaign. Many have validation features to confirm that a customer actually meant to sign up for your list. This is a great way to reduce spam, and to make sure your subscriber really wants to hear from you. Popular e-mail marketing services include:

- Constant Contact: *www.constantcontact.com*
- AWeber: *www.aweber.com*
- iContact: *www.icontact.com*
- Infusionsoft: *www.infusionsoft.com*

Such services have an autoresponder feature that is designed to send a series of messages to people who sign up for your list. The *Harvard Business Review* says most people only buy after the seventh contact from you. I suggest you set up an autoresponder sequence with at least ten messages to be sent over sixty to ninety days.

All e-mail marketing services charge a monthly fee, which is either based on the number of people on your list, or the number of e-mails sent each month. The costs for a CRM system can range from $19.95 to $395 per month based on the capabilities of the system you get. Check out *www.SmallBizCRM.com* for more information.

EMERSON'S essentials

Permission is perishable. *Once someone gives you his or her e-mail address there's a clock that is ticking on your relationship. You must keep your list engaged. Communicate with your list at least quarterly, monthly if you can.*

The CAN-SPAM Act

E-mail marketing is subject to regulation by the government. The CAN-SPAM Act of 2003 requires that you give recipients an unsubscribe method, that you identify yourself as a business, that the subject line of your e-mails is not misleading, and that you provide the postal address of your business. If you receive an opt-out request, you must comply within ten days.

It is also critical to publish a privacy policy on your site to assure people that their contact information is safe and will not be sold or distributed.

EMERSON'S action steps

[1] Identify your target customer and have a list of keywords before you start using any social media site or developing any content for the web.

[2] Develop five ways to attract potential and current customers to sign up for your mailing list.

[3] Keep your list engaged. Communicate with your list at least quarterly or monthly, if possible.

[4] Use your blog to establish yourself as an expert in your field.

15

CULTIVATE THE MARKET

$$\left[\text{ Six months before you start } \right]$$

One of your most valuable skills as an entrepreneur is the ability to make friends and win people over. People do business with people they like and people they know. Hopefully, you can be both to your clients. There are many businesses like yours, but one thing that separates your company from others is who you know and how you know them.

The Thirty-Second Commercial

Before you hit the street extolling the virtues of your great product or service, it is crucial that you have a clear thirty-second commercial (also known as "the elevator pitch") for your business. I've spoken about this earlier in Chapter 11, but now I'm going to discuss it in more detail.

When someone asks you what you do, you need to have a crisp and memorable response that makes it clear what business you are in and how you solve problems for your customers. Your commercial is intended for very brief, chance encounters. It is important because it helps you make a lasting first impression. You use it to showcase your professionalism, the benefits you provide, and your expertise. The goal is to capture your target's attention and interest so that you can engage them in a more substantial and meaningful way.

A strong thirty-second commercial will help you create better networking connections, and it can draw people to you. People will seek you out if you present yourself *and* your business professionally.

All thirty-second commercials must convey the following:

- Your unique selling position
- Credibility boosts, such as clients, revenues, or awards
- Your relevant background
- Your target market
- Your enthusiasm

EMERSON'S experience

Here is my thirty-second pitch: "My name is Melinda Emerson. I am an author, small business coach, and social media strategist. I specialize in helping people transition from a job to starting a business. I have worked with thousands of entrepreneurs since I started coaching business owners more than six years ago. I also consult with *Fortune* 100 corporations that want to sell to small business customers. Are you a full-time entrepreneur or a closet entrepreneur?"

Here are some secrets on delivering your thirty-second commercial:

- You must capture your target's attention in the *first seven seconds* or you will fail.
- Lead with your most compelling, attention-grabbing two lines. It is essential to establish credibility.
- Use your background, clients, awards, or anything that "validates" you to your target.
- Close with a question or call to action. Examples of calls to action include: Would you like to talk further? Over lunch perhaps? What day is good next week to give you a call? Do you know anyone who might need my services?

EMERSON'S essentials

Friendly conversation can always turn into a potential business lead. *Whenever you attend networking functions or, for that matter, go anywhere, you should always have business cards.*

Be prepared

When it comes to networking, you never know where you might meet someone who can help you grow your business, so it pays to always be prepared with plenty of business cards. It's like that old saying goes, "Never leave home without them."

An accountant once told me that the rule of thumb is that you should go through roughly 500 business cards every two months when you first start a business. I even carry business cards to the hair salon, because you never know who's in the shampoo bowl next to you.

EMERSON'S essentials

The networking cocktail hour before any event *is* the event. *Be early for the reception so you can circulate. Once you sit down to dinner, the only people you can network with are the other nine people at your table.*

The follow-up

The way to build relationships is through continued contact. It is essential to follow up within two weeks after meeting with a potential business contact. You can do this in multiple ways. The quickest and easiest way is e-mail. I prefer to send a handwritten note on my company stationery, since I feel this adds a personal touch. You can have note-card stationary printed with your company logo on it.

Secondly, send your company collateral materials and a work sample with a formal cover letter. Once you send a marketing packet, follow that with a call within seven business days. If you do not reach your target, send an e-mail in addition to leaving a voicemail. After that initial follow-up, your third step should be to make an appointment to talk about any pressing business problems the contact might be having. When appropriate, inquire about potential opportunities or any connections your new contact might be able to send your way. As well, ask if you can do a capabilities presentation.

Once you have your face-to-face meeting with the potential client, even if there's no opportunity apparent, a call or note every quarter is appropriate. Add them to your holiday card list and be sure to invite them if you have any special events like an open house, opening night at a local theatre performance, or your company's holiday party. You never know—they just might come. If you earn one contract from just one of your attendees, it could cover the cost of your event. Remember, you must spend money to make money.

EMERSON'S experience

Take the time to listen and respect people no matter who they are. You can learn something from anyone. You never really know in advance how someone can help you—and most importantly, help your business.

Early on in my first business, I was hosting a reception as a sponsor of the ballet. I was excited because there was a potential client whom I had been trying to get to notice my firm, and I knew she was a huge fan of the ballet. I called her office and invited her and her husband to join me at the ballet and attend my pre-reception. To my delight, she accepted my invitation.

The day before the reception, as I sat in the hair salon, my cell phone rang. The facility staff informed me that I would not be allowed to have food in the reception area, and that the time had been scaled back for the event. I completely panicked.

When I got off the phone, my hair stylist asked me which theatre was hosting the performance. When I told her, she said, "I think I can help you." It turned out that her brother-in-law was the lawyer for the theatre. She made two phone calls, and I suddenly had no more problems. My event went off perfectly; my guests had a lovely time, and I finally got an audience with my elusive client. It pays to be nice to people.

Look for ways to meet people

Encounters with people you don't know are important. Look at it this way: You don't meet strangers; you meet friends you just don't know yet. There are a few rules to this kind of networking.

Always invite the person to talk about themselves first. After all, the more you know about them, the better you can tailor your thirty-second pitch. Be ready with your short commercial about your business. Consider this your opportunity to make a positive first impression.

It is very important that you sound excited about what you do when you talk to people. You are always selling the business and yourself. Be careful never to tie up someone for more than fifteen minutes unless the contact seems to want to prolong the conversation.

Trains, planes, and buses are a great way to meet other business people. I only take the Amtrak Acela express train, which is how most business travelers in the Northeast ride. When I ride the train, I look for an open seat next to someone who looks like a businessperson. You just never know who could be a high-ranking executive, so I keep my mind and my options open. I try to make a friend or at least to learn something from someone during the ride. Most of the time, I accomplish both goals.

EMERSON'S experience

I was on the train to New York City for a meeting. I raced for the taxicab line and stood behind an older gentleman. He was a handsome man with unusually smooth skin, white hair, and a beard, sixty-some years of age. He was dressed in jeans and a suede vest—not exactly normal business attire—but he had the most unique leather briefcase I had ever seen. It was so nice-looking that I complimented him on it.

He said that someone on his sales staff had given it to him for Christmas. Following on my interest, I asked, "So what brings you to the Big Apple?"

He told me he had some business and a meeting with his brother. As we continued our conversation—the line was moving slow that day—I learned he was the founder and CEO of one of the top

African-American hair care companies on the East Coast. It was pouring down rain, and I told him I was worried about being late for my meeting, so we shared a cab. He seemed interested in my budding business and paid for the cab ride. More importantly, he gave me his card and asked me to contact his company about doing business. I followed up with him within a week after our meeting.

Build personal networks

When I first moved to Philadelphia, I put my nose to the grindstone for a few years to build up my career, then I turned my attention to meeting people. I did three things. First, I joined the Urban League Young Professionals Organization to do volunteer work, socialize, and participate in professional development activities. Then I found a church home. The third thing I did was to reach out to the alumni association of my alma mater, Virginia Tech. These three associations paid off in spades years later when I started my business. My first customers came from those associations.

EMERSON'S action steps

[1] Be ready with your thirty-second commercial about your business.

[2] You must capture your target's attention in the *first seven seconds.*

[3] Lead with your most compelling, attention-grabbing two lines.

[4] Never go anywhere without business cards.

[5] Talk to anyone. You never know how they might be able to help you and your business.

16

SETTING UP SHOP

$$\left[\ \textit{Six months before you start}\ \right]$$

Where do you plan to locate your business? World headquarters
for many multimillion-dollar businesses started on a kitchen table,
on a corner desk in a bedroom, in a basement, or in a garage. Great
ideas and ambition can percolate just about anywhere. What is most
important is the vision and hard work of the entrepreneur. Success can change your geography over time from a kitchen table to a
boardroom, but what do you need to get started? Here are some rules
to consider:

1. **Let the business growth drive your expansion.** Keep your
    overhead as low as possible. Run your business from your
    house or apartment until it becomes almost impossible to keep
    up with sales and inventory in the space you have (watch out
    for zoning regulations, however; they might cause problems).

2. **Get a business address.** Do not use your home address for your business. Rent a mailbox at a UPS store, which will give you a real street address. You can also purchase a P.O. box from the local post office. When my business started to grow, I got scary letters from strange people and prisoners at my home address. People also dropped by unannounced looking for work. As well, I got—and still get—an incredible amount of small business junk mail.

3. **If you can't do business from home, look for inexpensive space.** One source is the National Business Incubation Association (NBIA), a private, nonprofit, 501(c)(3) membership organization. It's considered the world's leading organization for advancing business incubation and entrepreneurship. Its mission is to provide training for small business people and a clearinghouse for information on incubator management and development issues and on tools for assisting start-up and fledgling firms. Their website is *www.nbia.org.*

Other sources include state-, county-, and city-sponsored business incubators that are designed to promote and support small businesses. Get all of the information you can so you can get the right space at the right price. Look for business owners with excess space to sublet or share a few days a week. I have a coaching client who is a therapist who only sees patients three times a week in the evenings, so she shares space with a dermatologist who stops seeing patients at 4 P.M. each day.

4. **Invest in a good computer and back-up system.** Start with a good laptop with a wireless connection for the Internet and your printer. Whenever you buy a computer or any electronics for your business, get the three-year crash-and-burn

platinum warranty. You cannot afford to have your computer down for one hour and certainly not three days. Purchase a thumb drive or an external drive to back up your files. Your computer is your "brains in a box"—it can help to write proposals, e-mail customers, track your budget and sales, manage subcontractors, allow you to order stuff over the Internet, look up information, create and monitor your task lists, and a ton of other stuff. A good computer with the Microsoft Office Suite of software, high-speed Internet access, 8 GB of RAM, and a Terabyte (1,000 GB) hard drive should get you started. You can get what you need for between $800 and $1200.

Be on the lookout for sales and special deals. Between Christmas and the end of the year, when retailers are trying to clear their inventories, is a great time to buy electronics for your business. Salespeople are often willing to make you a deal after the holidays so they will get their bonus. Save all receipts; you can write off the purchase against your taxes for the year. Talk to your accountant about how much of an investment you need to make in your business. Remember, only spend what's in your financial plan's budget.

5. **Store your stuff.** You need a home for accounting records, receipts, bills of lading, order forms, invoices, brochures, tax information, incorporation information, and lots of other paperwork. A four-drawer file cabinet, hanging file folders, regular file folders, and a sense of order are just the ticket, especially if the IRS ever audits you. Keep your personal and business information separate to minimize confusion and to simplify your operation. It also makes it easier for you or your bookkeeper to track spending and receipts and determine whether you are actually making money. When you make a bank deposit, write on the

deposit receipt whom the check was from and the amount. Get a fireproof safe to store blank checks, important papers, and any software that you've purchased. Make a copy of all checks from clients. When you pay invoices, it is a good idea to record the date and check number you used on the invoice to assist your bookkeeper with the financial records.

6. **Buy second-hand when you can.** Opportunities to buy used or refurbished desks, tables, chairs, bookshelves, and other equipment are everywhere. I love *www.freecycle.org* and *www .craigslist.com* for this kind of stuff. Freecycle.org is a cool website where people who don't want things post notices to give them away for free. Their mission is to build a worldwide gifting movement in order to reduce waste. In many cases, you will save up to 75–80 percent off retail.

Look around for the best quality you can find. There are plenty of second-hand furniture stores. Talk to friends who still work in the corporate world and find out if they know of companies selling used furniture. When I first started my business, my brother worked for Dupont. They had a sale of old furniture. We shopped for my first file cabinets there, and got some great deals. Just make sure that the drawers work, the legs are securely attached to all chairs, and that it's reasonably clean. Measure your available space to make sure what you're buying fits. The time to buy new will come later when you start to make money.

7. **Plan how you will communicate.** How will your customers reach you? A cell phone can be a virtual office, giving access to you anytime or any place. But the signal can be weak or disrupted, giving the customer a less-than-professional impression of your business. Make sure you have a good landline

phone with the capacity for up to four incoming lines (even if you are starting with just one line). Get a professional headset so you can multitask.

Create a voice mailbox and make sure the greeting you record is polished and professional. You may also want to invest in an 800 number. Other communications devices you may need include a PDA, cell phone, and fax machine. Remember, your phone is the lifeline to sales. You want to be easy to do business with. Get free estimates from your local phone company and other providers to see who has the best deals. Look for service packages that offer the biggest discounts. Also, be aware of termination fees and contract requirements.

8. **Purchase a business insurance policy for your new assets.** If you rent office space, secure a business property insurance policy. Even if you work from home you will need a separate policy for your business assets. You will also need liability insurance to protect you from a lawsuit should any of your products or services result in someone being injured or property being damaged. Your vendors will typically require a copy of your liability policy to be included with an RFP form. Some even require that they be listed as additionally insured on your policy.

If you have employees you will also need Workman's Compensation insurance. This will protect you and your employees should anyone be hurt on the job. The cost of this insurance is high, but it varies based on the types of workers you have and the level of risk involved in their job function. I have found that the cheapest option for Workman's Compensation is to buy it from your state. Regardless, you *must* have Workman's Compensation insurance if you have employees. It's the law.

Leasing as an Option

Consider leasing office equipment instead of buying it. There are several advantages to this strategy, the most important being an improvement in your cash position. A loan to purchase equipment requires at least 25 percent of the loan in cash upfront. Other than a refundable security deposit, equipment leases require no money down. Additional benefits include:

Easier financing than a purchase. Leasing companies typically want a year or less of business credit history before approving a furniture or office equipment lease. Capital equipment loans require three years of financial history.

Leasing means you will not be stuck with obsolete equipment. You can do a short-term lease, which swaps out the equipment every one to two years. There's always a faster, cheaper model coming out for copiers, printers, and postage meters. If you lease a copier, make sure you really need it. If you pay the lease fee as well as a per-copy fee, it might be cheaper to go to the corner stationery store to make your copies.

Leasing helps the bottom line in more ways than one. Your accountant may be able to re-categorize some assets on your balance sheet. Your firm's debt-to-equity ratio will look much healthier, as will your earnings-to-fixed-assets ratio. Keep in mind that the lease contract will be reported as assets on your balance sheet and taxes under certain types of agreements.

When leasing office equipment:

- Shop around for the best financing deal
- Make sure you can break the lease agreement if you have to. Note the cost of the penalty fee.

- Don't lease for more than two years
- Look for an option-to-buy clause
- Negotiate a "modern equipment substitution clause" that lets you trade up for the latest technology

EMERSON'S action steps

[1] Let your business drive your growth; work from home until the business operations require professional office space.

[2] Get your first office space on the cheap. Look for a small business incubator, or sublet or share space with another entrepreneur who has a similar business or works opposite hours.

[3] Create an internal communications plan (phone, voicemail, Internet, cell phone with e-mail ability).

[4] Store your important records and receipts properly so you can find them later when you need them.

[5] Buy used when you can. Consider leasing office equipment, but run the numbers to make sure it's a good deal.

[6] Get yourself a business address other than your home.

[7] Get yourself a good computer with a three-year crash-and-burn warranty. Don't go cheap! This is the brain of your business.

[8] Look into all the business insurance that you may need: property, liability, health, and Workman's Compensation.

17

BUILD YOUR TEAM

$$\left[\ \textit{Five months before you start}\ \right]$$

When you can no longer survive as an "army of one," it is time to bring in reinforcements . . . employees. Hiring and working with employees will be an adjustment, but it's one you will thank yourself for later, particularly if you choose well.

One of the first skills you must learn as an entrepreneur is to *delegate*. Figure out what tasks you can afford to have someone else take care of for you. Your time is too valuable to spend doing basic follow-up and mailings. In a small business, resources are always tight, so it's important to get the most out of them. The same is true of your employees. If you do not use your employees' full potential, you are wasting money. Pay as high a wage as you can and communicate with them upfront about your long-term goals. Nothing is worse then hiring an employee who leaves two months later because he really didn't see himself with your company for the long term.

A second important skill you must develop is the art of treating your employees differently from one another. They are not all the same kind of person. You must learn to communicate with them in a way in which they can hear you, so that you can achieve *your* goals through their work. If you hire relatives, this will take on even greater importance. Managing family can be tricky. The people closest to you may have trouble seeing you as the boss. In those cases, you may need to over-communicate until things gel.

EMERSON'S essentials

Different generations bring different attitudes toward work. *In order to be an effective manager, you need to educate yourself on how to effectively communicate across the generations as well as cultures.*

What Kind of Employee Do You Want?

The obvious answer is the hardest-working, most conscientious individual you can find at the lowest possible cost. You want someone who is willing to work when you need her. But first, you need to really understand the staffing needs of your business. Whether it be sales coverage for the hours you have the doors open, a delivery person, a helper, technical support staff, or someone to answer phones, you must know how many hours you need them, the skills required of them, and the duration of the position. These are keys to making the right hiring decisions.

The job description
One of the first things you must do, once you have considered what kind of help you need, is to write a detailed job description. I prefer to write down everything the employee could possibly be asked to

do so she or he can be clear about how big the job is from the start. A good job description is key to helping an employee do her job effectively. It will also clearly communicate your expectations of job performance. You can also use the document as the basis for your job review.

- Create an exhaustive list of job tasks, then prioritize them. Try not to be overwhelming, just accurate.
- Divide the list into three categories: critical tasks, routine tasks, and occasional tasks.
- Keep your job description to a page. (You do not want to scare away the person you are trying to hire.)

Once you have a job description, you must evaluate what kind of person you need to fulfill all these duties. There are several categories of employee that might meet your requirements:

Full-time. A full-time employee generally works forty hours a week and is paid overtime for hours worked over forty. You must pay Social Security, disability, and federal and state taxes for each such employee you hire. However, you have options as to whether you provide health, vacation, or retirement benefits. In many cases, the benefits you provide will depend on the labor pool you're hiring from. If the skill set you require of an employee is scarce, be prepared to offer a competitive salary and benefit packages to attract the best talent.

Part-time. A part-time employee generally works from fifteen to thirty hours per week and can be a solid asset in covering hours such as nights and weekends, when your business might need to provide customer service support during off-hours. Part-time help can provide great flexibility in meeting increased sales activity or in addressing a surge in call volumes. Most importantly, part-time staffing permits you to adjust worker schedules to reflect the needs of your business. The primary downside is that you may be competing with their full-time positions and you may not always get the hours you need from them. Generally, you do not have to pay either medical or retirement benefits to part-time employees, but this also depends on the skills you require and the state of the labor pool.

Temporary. A temporary worker, often hired through an agency, can usually be on the job within a few hours and quickly help you meet an increase in business needs. Changing lifestyles and increased mobility in recent years have made temporary work very attractive to many highly skilled people.

An agency can shorten the time and expense of recruiting, screening, interviewing, and checking on prospective employees. The major downside to using such employees is that their training and orientation are often lost when that worker moves on. Additionally, these workers cost you a bit more than an hourly employee would. You also cannot expect the same level of loyalty or dedication to your business that you would expect from a permanent employee.

Contractors. These workers, known as freelancers or 1099 employees, can be very valuable in meeting your business needs, especially short-term, complex ones, without adding to payroll. They work for a straight hourly rate and are responsible for their own payroll taxes. If you pay a contractor over $600 you are required to send a 1099 tax form to them and the IRS to report their income. You define the scope and timing of the project that you want done, negotiate the price, and specify the benchmarks.

Once the project is done, the contractor moves on. If you want to keep him on for a project expansion, you may have to renegotiate, and this could cost you. You can start off your employees as contractors on a project basis to see if you like their work style and performance. This will ease your budget since you won't have to pay benefits and taxes immediately, and you can get rid of problem employees before they can file for unemployment benefits.

Interns. College students working toward their degrees are often encouraged or required to participate in internship and co-op programs that relate to their field of study. This can be a low- or no-cost source of labor for your company. In return for their labor, you give them college credits and experience in your business.

You must create some ground rules, such as the length of time they must work per week. Establish a dress code: no jeans, sneakers, or piercings, etc. It's also good if you can give them a specific project to do by the time they are finished with their internship. If you give them a specific project, whenever there's down time they can work on that project. Try to assign them projects that will test their skills, teach them new skills, and bring value to your business.

Internships occur during the school year or over the summer or winter break periods. Co-op students are with the business a longer period of time. Many co-op students expect to be paid, but they will be around for six months.

Providing internships and co-op opportunities is a great way of establishing working relationships with local colleges and key faculty members, which could also give you access to some low-cost consulting assistance.

The Selection Process

Choosing the right person for a job can be a challenge. As the owner and sole employee of the business, you are the personnel department and will have to decide whether the potential hire will be a help or a hindrance.

What kinds of skills do you expect to find in your potential hire? If you are looking for a salesperson and your candidate is not outgoing and seems wary of strangers, he may not be the best candidate for that position. If you are looking for someone with technical skills in graphics or computer-aided design and she is unfamiliar with the programs and lingo associated with that profession, you may have a problem.

Like anything else in business, I like to get referrals for employees. I send job descriptions out to everyone in my personal e-mail database to see if someone I know can send me a great candidate. I also use job-listing websites including *www.craigslist.com* and *www.elance.com* to find employees, and I reach out to career services advisors for recent college graduates. A poor selection process costs you both time and money and can be unfair to the person you select.

In your job description, you've listed and prioritized the needed skills. The more interviews you conduct, the more you will be able to distinguish between those who are merely good at interviewing and those who are the best fit for your company.

The employment application

One great source of screening information is the application for employment that the candidate completes before the interview. Standard blank applications are available on the Internet.

Make sure the form you use includes space for the candidate to give his or her name, address, phone, and Social Security number; educational data for all schools attended, degrees, diplomas, certifications; criminal background data, arrest records, felony convictions;

professional references with names, titles, contact information, and the period of employment.

Going over these applications, you'll be able to easily reject the people whose skill sets don't match your requirements or who are unqualified for some other reason. From the remainder, select the best. They're your interview pool.

Ask the candidates who interview to sign forms giving your firm permission to check their credit report or perform a drug screening. The vendors who perform these services can provide the appropriate release forms.

The final step before the interviews is to prepare questions that will give you some insight into the personality and attitude of the candidates. The answers you get will really help you round out your impression of them.

Here are some questions you should ask:

> Tell me about your work experience.
> Why did you apply for this job?
> What do you know about our company?
> What are your long-term goals for your career?
> What do you see yourself doing five years from now?
> What is your most important accomplishment to date?
> What motivates you?
> Describe your favorite and worst boss and why.
> Why should I hire you?
> Have you ever had a conflict with a co-worker? How did you resolve it?
> Describe a time when you had to multitask while handling a major project?
> Have you ever worked in a small business environment?

There are five things to keep in mind when conducting an interview:

1. Be a good listener.
2. Know how to redirect a conversation.
3. Take notes during the interview.
4. Go with your gut instinct (if something doesn't feel right, it's not right).
5. The candidate is also interviewing you, so be ready to answer questions.

Putting People on Payroll

Now that you're employing people, get ready for some serious record-keeping. When you add employees, you also add a paperwork burden to your business. You must make sure that you have W-2 and W-9 forms updated annually on all full-time and 1099 contract employees. Your accountant can handle the basic payroll taxes—FICA, state taxes, Social Security deductions, disability contributions, and others. Talk with your accountant, lawyer, and/or payroll service before hiring anyone. Systems must be in place before you have employees working for you. You can go to jail faster for not paying payroll taxes than for not paying income taxes.

Payroll companies

A great source for help in making your hiring process compliant with the law is to use a payroll company. Some factors to consider when choosing a company are:

Responsiveness. If there are mistakes with payroll, how quickly can it be corrected and paychecks be re-issued?

Easy communication. How hard is it for the company to add a new employee to your system? Updating the payroll list should be quick and easy.

You will need to communicate with the payroll service regularly, so make sure they have qualified personnel to work with you.

EMERSON'S experience

Arrange to speak with the same person each time you call. One time my regular payroll clerk was on vacation, and her replacement accidentally processed a $50,000 paycheck for me. Nearly $28,000 in taxes was also pulled from my account, and it took me a week to get it straightened out. Shortly after, I switched payroll companies.

Ask for small business references and check them. Make sure the company is bonded and registered with the Better Business Bureau.

Basic monthly payroll services include: paycheck processing, online account access, quarterly tax filings, and direct deposit. Prices can range from $20 to $150 per month, depending on the frequency of payroll and the number of employees. Per-check fees, if applicable, range from $0.75 to $2 or more, and additional fees for adding new employees, check delivery, and extra reporting are typical. Make sure you get a full breakdown of all fees before you commit to a provider.

Offering Benefits

Next, you must define what benefits you are prepared to offer a new employee. Generally, the lower the employee rank, the lower the salary and the fewer the benefits. What you pay for employees is defined by the skills, experience, and education they need, as well as by what the competition is offering. Figure into your cost any perks you offer (free/subsidized education, paid sick time, numerous vacation days, rapid advancement, 401(k), etc.) The benefits you offer reflect the importance you place on attracting the right people. If you run a home health-care agency, you won't hire any registered nurses for minimum wage. If you are looking for a sales clerk, you may be able to start them at a low wage. Make sure you have a good idea what you will need to pay to get the talent you need.

EMERSON'S essentials

Stay-at-home moms looking to get back into the workforce appreciate flexibility. *Offering adaptable work schedules and virtual work can be a big incentive to qualified workers. Other possibilities include a compressed work week—four nine-hour days, or three twelve-hour days.*

What if you can't offer competitive benefits? How can you attract good help? One possibility is to offer potential employees the opportunity to share in the company's profits through direct stock ownership. Another possibility is a bonus program that will benefit everyone if certain goals are met.

EMERSON'S experience

In the early days of my business, I could not always pay my employees, but to make up for it, I allowed my staff to use my equipment and resources to do freelance work for other people. I also bought lunch and dinner every day (largely because we worked most nights until 9 P.M. or so). I would give them tokens or rides home from work every night. Whenever it was somebody's birthday, I always bought that person a nice gift. At the end of a hard contract, we would all go out to dinner at a nice restaurant with spouses and significant others.

I also allowed everyone to interview any potential hires. They all voted on any new hire, and the vote had to be unanimous before an offer was made, even for our interns. My rationale for this was that my core staff was the priority, and if a new person was going to disrupt the office vibe, they could not join the Quintessence family.

Job sharing is also a great way to get the help you need—two permanent part-time employees share one position. Also consider the possibility of a virtual employee. High-speed Internet service, e-mail, Skype, teleconferencing, fax machines, and same-day courier services have made the virtual office a reality. If you operate a customer service-based business, this may be a great solution to get a high-quality employee at reasonable cost.

Creating the Rules

Every business has rules, which need to be explained and followed by all employees so everyone understands your expectations. You should establish policies on insubordination, chronic lateness, laziness, excessive absenteeism, lying, theft, substance abuse, personal use of cell phones, and other personality issues. It is a good idea to ask new employees to sign a document or handbook outlining your guidelines. This cuts down on any confusion later and gives you legal protection in the event you have to fire an employee.

Reprimanding your employees

One of the hardest things to do in business is to reprimand a member of the staff. Have corrective conversations in a private setting, and list several positives before addressing the negative incident. I also make a point of highlighting anything I could have done differently that would have made the situation better. I always suggest that we all have something to learn in every situation.

EMERSON'S essentials

If you become a business owner who thinks you cannot learn anything new or does not make mistakes, be prepared for your staff to leave you. *Your competition will also soon overtake your market share. Shortsightedness will kill a business faster than a cash crunch.*

Hiring family members

Hiring family members may be your best source of inexpensive labor, but the tradeoffs can be dedication and attitude. The separation between work and your personal life can erode quickly, and both can suffer if the demands of your work leave no time for your personal priorities. Whether you are employing siblings, spouse, children, parents, cousins, or even very close friends, business conflicts can put enormous strain on relationships. Spouses and siblings working together need clearly defined roles. They should drive separate cars and have offices away from each other.

It's important that relatives be treated like everyone else in terms of pay and job title so that everything in your business can work together harmoniously. The best approach to minimize the inevitable pressures that result from working with family is communication, communication, and more communication.

The website *www.family-business-experts.com* provides excellent insight into the problems and solutions for family-managed businesses. Many of these solutions are low-cost or free.

Always take care of your people

There is honor in all work, so treat all employees with respect. Without them, your business would be in peril. Whenever I introduce a staff member to a client or anyone, I say, "They work with me" and not for me. It sounds better and is more accurate. I also empower my staff to give me feedback constantly. If I do something they find objectionable, I invite them to let me know. They're the source of much of the wisdom that I am imparting to you in this book.

One key thing I took away from my days in corporate America was: *People leave people, not jobs.* If I learned anything from my former managers, it was how *not* to treat people. Your staff is an extension of you. Be good to them. Treat them like family—although we all know that nobody's family is perfect.

EMERSON'S essentials

If you treat people like employees, that is how they will act. *If you nickel and dime people, they will do the same to you and to your business. Your employees will be more concerned about lunchtime or what time they get off than about what you are paying them to do and do well.*

Dealing with lateness

Be sure to have a policy regarding attendance and your business's core hours. At the same time, this is another area in which you need to employ flexibility. If you dock pay for every fifteen minutes of tardiness and give people a hard time when they need time off, chances are they'll call in sick on the day you need them the most. My philosophy about lateness and emergency time off is this: I am flexible as long as I know what is going on.

Turnover is expensive. The time it takes you to train the next employee could have been spent making money. Don't condone unprofessional behavior, but keep it in perspective. If your assistant, who always comes early and works hard, is late one day, don't say anything about it. People want to work for an employer who cares about them and values their contribution. Be careful not to bark orders and to leave "to do" lists for them. Say good morning. Ask them about their children or their weekend.

Whenever I hire anyone—even an intern—I give him or her a copy of my business plan. If I can get all of my staff to buy into what I am trying to do, they will be more understanding when money is tight or when we need to work until midnight to complete a project.

It's Just Not Working Out

Firing someone is a high-stress situation because often it signals that you have made a bad hiring decision. When your employee has not met your expectations or doesn't fit into your organization, it is time to say goodbye.

When an employee is terminated, it is usually one for of two reasons—an *immediate firing* for insubordination, theft, drug use, or illegal activity, or an *ongoing behavior termination*. Reasons for this could include chronic lateness, laziness, high absenteeism, incompetence, or poor attitude.

Both types of firings present legal challenges, which is why you should document their cause in detail.

Immediate firing. Document the specific behavior that is the cause of termination—when it occurred, where, witnesses (if any), and cite the specific passages in your company handbook or code of conduct that it violates.

Ongoing behavior. Note each instance of the behavior that is grounds for the termination. Document that you asked the employee for specific improvements and note the timeframe in which these were to be met. The time you set can be a week, a month, or more depending on how serious you consider the problem.

Your documentation can help you significantly if the employee files a lawsuit or in case you need to fight a claim for unemployment.

When informing the employee of your decision to terminate their relationship with your company, stick to the facts. Don't show emotion—even though you'll probably be feeling it. Terminate with kindness and in privacy. Arrange for the employee to return all company property, including keys and IDs.

Regardless of how employees leave your organization, whether voluntarily or involuntarily, you should always conduct an exit interview. The exit interview should be calm and professional. Details of the interview are important, so carefully note each point made in the discussion. Every time an employee leaves your organization, try to learn something you can do better.

EMERSON'S action steps

[1] Write a detailed job description to clarify what skills you need.

[2] Create an employee handbook so everyone knows the rules.

[3] Hire a payroll service to keep things simple.

[4] Tread lightly when hiring family members. You could lose your business and the relationship.

[5] Keep a paper trail on all disciplinary meetings with staff.

[6] If an employee doesn't work out, consider what role you played in his failure.

18

SET UP CUSTOMER SERVICE SYSTEMS

[*Three months before you start*]

Before you generate your first sale, you need to think about customer service. What are your customer service policies going to be? Are all sales final, will you issue store credit, or will you offer a money-back guarantee on your product or service? All businesses must have a customer service policy for the telephone or e-mail inquiries.

You must train your staff in how to greet and assist customers, and all employees need to know how to handle unhappy customers. In these days of increasing global competition, customer service can provide your competitive edge.

Companies that are focused on building long-term relationships know what customers need, want, and expect. This is the core benefit of excellent customer service. Your competitors will bombard your best customers with reasons they should drop your company and start doing business with them: lower costs for comparable service, a wider array of services for the same cost, or the use of newer technologies. But if you provide good customer service, you'll be able to retain your customer base.

Why is this important? Keeping existing customers is cheaper than trying to get new ones. A recent survey published by Accenture reported that 59 percent of customers surveyed switched at least one service provider due to poor service.

Cost is not everything. Customers want their needs taken care of, and often they're willing to pay a bit more for better service.

EMERSON'S experience

When I was a kid, my dad worked a second job as a part-time salesman at Sears. One year around Christmas, a man who looked like he worked all day on a construction site walked into the electronics department.

The man was dirty and muddy and still had his work boots on. My dad noticed that no one was waiting on him. Clearly the other salespeople had made assumptions about this customer based on how he looked.

This was back in the 1980s when camcorders had just come on the market. The man wanted to see how those new machines worked. My dad did a full demonstration and even moved the machine so the man could see himself on TV in the showroom.

At the end of the demonstration the man said, "I'm not going to buy anything tonight; I want my wife to see this too. When is the next time you'll be working?"

When my dad clocked in the following Sunday, the man and his wife were waiting for him—this time cleaned up and smartly dressed.

After another demonstration, the man bought ten camcorders. It turned out he owned a construction company. He bought a camcorder for every member of his family for Christmas.

It wasn't only his family that had a good holiday. My dad's commission on that sale was $1,500. That night Dad sat my brothers and me down and told us never to judge a book by its cover and always to treat everyone with respect. That was my first customer service lesson.

Under-Promise and Over-Deliver

Delivering more than what you promised is a good way to build customer rapport—both outside and inside your company. Likewise, doing it sooner than expected makes a strong impression.

Successful companies make a habit of exceeding customer expectations. I recently took my car into the dealership to get an oil change, and to check out an interior light that was not working properly. The service area was crowded that day, and I expected at least a two-hour wait. To my surprise, not only did the service people do the oil change, they also replaced the bulb and put in new windshield wipers (I had asked the service advisor to "take a look at the wipers for me")—all in an hour! Best of all, the wipers and light were done at no charge. They did more than I expected, and I could not have been more pleased. The dealership created a positive link between their brand and me and reinforced the customer relationship. I'll remember this experience when I buy my next car.

Solve your customer's problem

If you can't put your finger on your customer's problem, you won't solve it. Worse, you will waste time and lose credibility. You must describe the problem clearly, and do it from the customer's point of view. To find out what the problem is, ask the right questions and listen before you act. Here are some approaches that are very effective:

Ask the customer what would solve the problem. Many times their requests can be surprisingly reasonable and relatively inexpensive. If the cause of the problem is clearly your product's failure, refund the customer's money or replace it.

Be courteous. Eighty percent of Americans believe that lack of courtesy is a problem in the United States. By focusing on basic courtesy with your employees, you can set yourself apart from the competition, especially since so many potential customers are not accustomed to it.

Be flexible. Even if you know the customer's complaint is suspect, negotiate with him or her, perhaps for partial credit toward a replacement purchase or a reduced or complimentary service. Reduce the areas of conflict that keep you from getting to an amicable solution.

EMERSON'S essentials

In business, it's cheaper to keep the customer. *Do not argue with customers about their opinion. It's bad for your blood pressure and bad for business. And in the long run, you won't win.*

The last and least attractive option in any customer dialogue is to just say no—but sometimes you have to do it. Managing difficult customers is part of the territory when you open a business. When it seems like nothing that you do is right, forget about preserving the relationship—preserve your sanity instead. If you have a client who just won't be satisfied, no matter what you do, let them go. Work hard to save the relationships that you can. Take great care of customers who love your work and acknowledge your dedication and professionalism. They are the backbone of your long-term business success.

Use customer relationship management (CRM) software

In Chapter 14, I talked about using CRM software to build and manage contact information about your customers. Some of the same database software also enables you to easily find and store information about clients, such as how often they buy and how much they spend with your business over a certain period. You not only have the latest sales history, but any service problems and future purchase considerations can all be in one place. When that customer calls, anyone with access to your CRM system will be an instant expert on that customer's history. This information will enable you to provide high-quality, low-cost customer service. Proper management of all interactions with the customer increases customer loyalty and provides a higher level of professionalism in your interactions. The higher your customer satisfaction, the better your customer retention, which means repeat business!

Customer Feedback Equals Customer Satisfaction

Collecting customer feedback to measure customer satisfaction with your company's performance is a way for you to proactively get information on how a customer values your products and services. Customer satisfaction surveys are the most accurate barometers to predict the success of a company because they directly ask customers about the critical success factors of your business. If done effectively, satisfaction surveys can deliver powerful incisive information and provide ways to gain a competitive edge. When measuring customer satisfaction, you can gather critical feedback about questions such as these:

- How satisfied are you with the purchase you made?
- How satisfied are you with the service you received?
- How likely are you to buy from us again?

Most surveys ask customers to rate their experiences in these areas on a numbered scale. With enough feedback from your customers, you can get a pretty good idea about how you are doing. If the results are not good, you've got work to do. For a sample customer satisfaction survey, see Appendix A.

EMERSON'S action steps

[1] Treat your customers well, and they will not only follow you, but they will sell for you by sharing their experience with others.

[2] Know your customer's needs, wants, and motives.

[3] Don't argue with your customers. You can't win.

[4] Work hard to save the relationships that you can. A bad reputation travels fast.

[5] Make sure you and your staff treat all your customers with courtesy. Even something this simple can set you apart from the competition.

[6] Use customer feedback to make changes and improve your business.

19

TAKING STOCK OF THINGS: IS EVERYTHING IN PLACE?

$$\left[\text{ \textit{One month before you start} }\right]$$

You have been extremely busy assembling all of the elements to get your business started—the idea, the support, the financing, the location, the marketing plan, and most of all, nurturing your confidence to make it all happen. As with any big plan, there are usually little details that must be addressed at the last minute. You don't want a small issue to prevent or delay your launch.

Here is a list of the top twenty items to check on in the weeks leading up to your launch. Make sure your bases are covered before your opening day.

- ❏ I've registered for an EIN number with the IRS and opened a business bank account.
- ❏ I've obtained required business licenses and permits and checked on zoning regulations.

- ❑ I've set up a business filing system.
- ❑ I've purchased a fireproof safe to store checks, software, and critical documents.
- ❑ I've ordered professional signage and collateral materials, all of which have my logo and contact information on them.
- ❑ I've purchased a supply of business forms such as sales slips, order forms, and blank receipts.
- ❑ I've purchased or leased and set up all the equipment I'll need, e.g., cash register, copiers, computers, printer, fax machine, postage meter.
- ❑ I've established an on-call agreement with a technology consultant.
- ❑ I've hired a lawyer to draft templates for contract agreements, mutual nondisclosure agreements, etc.
- ❑ I've hired a bookkeeper or accountant to set up accounting software and provide monthly support.
- ❑ I've conducted background checks and bonding on anyone handling money or merchandise.
- ❑ I've made sure phone lines are operating and voicemail systems have a professional and business-like message.
- ❑ I've ordered a credit card machine and applied for a merchant service account.
- ❑ I've carried out an orientation for my employees and trained cashiers how to use the credit card machines.
- ❑ I've made up and distributed weekly/monthly employee work schedules.
- ❑ I've sent out invitations to a grand opening event.
- ❑ I've set up a website with an online merchant service account to accept payments.
- ❑ I've launched advertising in print and online media.
- ❑ I've made sure news releases announcing the launch are ready to send to local publications and publish on the website.

❑ I've got a presence on Facebook, Twitter, LinkedIn, and any other useful social media sites where I can spread the word about my business.

Go through this list and make sure you've put a check next to each item. If need be, push back the date of your opening to give yourself time to get all your ducks lined up. While it's not good to delay the opening of your business, it's far worse to open with tasks left undone. Those skipped items will come back to haunt you in the weeks and months to come if you neglect them now.

Getting the Basics Right

The list above is primarily concerned with the launch of your business. But as we've seen, there are other things you need that have more to do with the day-to-day running of your business. They include:

Set up your customer service system. In Chapter 18 I discussed the importance of great customer service. Make sure your employees are aware of how to handle unhappy customers. Do your people have the power to make a customer refund or do all adjustments need to be made by you? Having a clear set of rules upfront will make your job easier.

■ **Manage the money.** In Chapter 7, I talked about using accounting software to track all sales, invoices, receipts, and any payroll. You should also keep physical copies of all receipts, invoices, and canceled checks. Set up a shredder to destroy credit card information to prevent theft or fraud. The system for managing your finances should make it easy to see income and expenses monthly and ease the creation of tax documents.

Firm up your vendor relationships. If you are selling services and your business experiences rapid growth, you can use temporary help such as freelancers, consultants, or interns or you can expand the hours of your staff. However, if you are selling a product and there is a dramatic rise in demand, you may need your suppliers to extend enough credit to help you meet demand. Keep your suppliers in the loop about your needs, and pay them as promptly as you can. The key to building a solid vendor relationship is early, frequent, and upfront communication. These people will be essential to the success of your operation.

- **Get your employee mix right.** Unless you are a solopreneur, your employees will be critical to your business success. The time to look at those folks, balance your workforce, and make sure you're hiring the best is before you open the doors, not after. To get the best employees, carefully look at work habits, enthusiasm, attitude, reliability, knowledge, and their common sense. A good hiring decision can save you grief once the doors are open and your business has launched. It's also a good habit to already know your next hire for every position in your business.
- **Create an emergency plan.** You should have an idea of who will run the business if you get sick or have to pull away from it for an extended time. Would you have to close shop, or do you have someone who could step in to cover until you come back. What is your "plan B"?

In the month before you launch, review these lists several times. You've spent twelve months getting to this place. Avoid any last-minute stumbles as you prepare for the greatest adventure of your life.

Part III

GO!

Sunday	Monday	Tuesday	Wednesday	Thursday	Friday	Saturday
				1	2	3
4	5	6	7	8	9	10
11	12	13	14	15	16	17
18	19	20	21	22	23	24
25	26	27	28	29	30	31

20

Launching Your Business

As the launch date of your business approaches, you must choose the best way to let the world know your new company is open for business. When you launch a business, the most important thing you must do is attract customers. With that as the goal, when you created your marketing plan you developed an advertising budget. This process included deciding which advertising vehicles you will use for your business launch.

For some businesses, certain advertising strategies aren't cost-effective and don't make sense. A neighborhood gas station probably doesn't need a TV campaign announcing its grand opening. On the other hand, a restaurant with multiple locations could benefit from running regional cable spots on television. Based on your target market, it is important to use the most appropriate advertising options.

Launch Strategies

Let's break down different launch strategies for generating sales leads and getting customers in the door.

Professional service businesses

If you are a professional service business, attracting clients is all about the face-to-face meeting. Professional services businesses typically have a longer sales cycle than retail businesses, where the sales come immediately with launch.

Often professional service businesses sell solutions, which means a significant amount of time is spent upfront understanding the challenge faced by a prospective customer. Lawyers, doctors, accountants, creative services firms, and technology firms are these types of enterprises.

At the start of your business, the work you've done in the previous year networking will be key. Call on your network to spread the word of your launch. Schedule meetings to do capabilities presentations. If your launch coincides with a trade show, consider distributing your news releases and marketing materials there, to announce that your company has entered the industry. The key thing to remember is that timely follow-up is essential to growing relationships.

EMERSON'S essentials

Never buy a booth the first year you attend a trade show. *Attending trade shows is expensive. Make sure that you are going to get a bang for your buck before you shell out cash to buy a booth space. Walk the show the first year, talk to exhibitors about their success rate, and make sure your target market potential is worth the investment.*

Online businesses

Generate buzz for your new business with a social media marketing campaign. Six months before you launch, you should increase your visibility on Twitter, LinkedIn, and Facebook. Once you are at your launch time, you should be even more visible. Set up a fact of the day about your industry or service. Use services like *www.hootsuite.com* or *www.cotweet.com* to postdate specific Twitter messages. It's like using a postdated check for your marketing tweets.

EMERSON'S essentials

Always remember the 4-to-1 rule in social media. *For every four postings on Twitter, Facebook, or any social media networking site, only one can be directly promoting your product or service.*

- Create an event on LinkedIn to invite your network to your grand-opening event.
- Have a site-warming party online. To attract visitors, use a thirty-day giveaway program and guest bloggers to bring awareness to your new business. To pull this off, you will probably need a social media strategist with influence to help.
- Comment on other blogs and participate in online forums to get attention.
- Post a helpful video for your audience on YouTube.
- Send out social media press releases as well as traditional news releases.
- Purchase pay-per-click advertising. Business typically bid on keyword phrases relevant to their target market. Google AdWords, Yahoo! Search Marketing, and Microsoft adCenter are the three largest network operators, and all three operate under a bid-based model. Depending on the size of your marketing budget, this could be a good move. You can be there instantly to solve the need of the potential customers. The

most important thing is to have the right search words so you attract the right customers.

Retail businesses

Success in retail is all about attracting a high volume of walk-in customers. As you launch your retail business, focus on providing neighborhood convenience, creating a unique shopping experience, and offering merchandise focused on the needs of your target customers. Here are some more retail promotional ideas:

- Offer special opening day discounts and specials to attract clients.
- Hire teens to hand out flyers.
- Partner with the other businesses in your area to do co-branded activities.
- Take out an ad on the table placemat at the local diner in your neighborhood.
- Consider putting a coupon in the community discount mailer or clipper magazine.
- A well-placed billboard a few blocks from your business can be effective as well.
- Purchase regional cable TV ads in the specific zip codes you serve.
- Purchase radio ads and have the radio station do a live broadcast from your location.

EMERSON'S essentials

Anyone will buy something once. *Your goal as a small business owner is to provide an outstanding customer experience to get your consumers to buy over and over again from you.*

For Any Business

Whether you're launching a consulting operation, an online business, or a neighborhood store, there are some things you can do to draw attention to your new business.

Host a grand opening. Offer giveaways and games for the entire family. Schedule a live remote with a local radio station that serves your target market. Offer great opening day specials and discount coupons for a return visit.

Develop a membership program. Create a frequent buyers club. Hold special sales and shopping hours and create special discounts. Sponsor a special event, e.g., a ballet or ball game to which customers get VIP tickets.

Update your website. Feature a countdown to your opening prominently on your home page. If you have a blog, develop a series of posts specifically about your business and expertise and launch.

Become a PR machine. If you can afford it, hire a publicist for the launch. You need to have a contact list for regional and national media to pitch. Develop three hooks to pitch your business to the media and don't forget the local business journal. Try one of these ideas:

- Create an exceptional guarantee.
- Try a sports gimmick, e.g. the company president will shave his head if the local football team wins.
- Develop a special sale item for the opening week with a portion of proceeds going to charity.
- Hire musicians to play in your store every Friday for a month after the launch.

- Throw some sort of contest for college students to create a jingle for the store or a YouTube commercial.

The day your business opens its doors will be one of unparalleled excitement for you. Be sure to get a good night's sleep before, because you're about to embark on a road that will be filled with long days and sometimes longer nights. But at the end is the incredible reward of becoming your own boss.

21

HANDLING CASH
AND YOUR BANK

One of the keys to controlling your cash management is being on top of your monthly financial statements. By the fifteenth of every month you should have a current balance sheet, profit and loss statement (P&L), and a statement of cash flows. These will tell you what your business did in terms of revenues and expenses for the previous month. Your bookkeeper or accounting clerk should produce these three financial statements for you each month. Falling behind in this paperwork is very dangerous to the health of your business. I have known too many business owners who waited until tax time to find out how their business did financially for the year.

So you don't get lost amid all the jargon, here are some basic definitions for you to keep in mind as your business proceeds:

- **Cash flow statement** is cash receipts minus cash payments from a given period.
- **Balance sheet** is a statement showing your company's financial position at the end of an accounting period.

- **Income statement** is your company's net income for the accounting period; also called a profit-and-loss statement.
- **Cost of goods sold** is the figure representing the cost of buying raw materials and producing finished goods.

In addition to the financial statements, you must track your expenses against your budget. All the trouble you went to in drawing up that budget will be wasted if you don't keep to it.

EMERSON'S essentials

You need accurate financial information to make good business decisions. *You must know how much each job or product costs you and what your profit margin was on that particular job or product. You also need up-to-date financial information so that you can effectively track your COGS (Cost of Goods Sold).*

In the fourth quarter of each year, you should prepare a budget and revenue projection for the next year. When preparing the budget, it is important to review your prior year's projected budget verses your actual expenses. This information will help you create a more accurate budget and assist you in reducing any out-of-control expenses.

Business taxes are due by March 15 of every year, not in April, like personal income taxes. Some business owners strategically delay paying business taxes until October. Talk with your tax preparer about whether you should file for an extension.

Ideas to Manage Cash Flow

The goal in cash-flow management is to hold on to your cash as long as you can. It is important that you not get a reputation as a business that does not pay its bills, but at the same time, it is essential to make sure that only priority bills are paid first. Develop a procedure for processing your accounts payable, or the bills of the business.

Set aside a regular day to write checks, such as every other Friday. You should never cut a check because you got a call from a vendor unless it's an emergency, and they are holding goods or services that your business needs. You must make sure you business always has enough cash to function.

Find out how your clients process invoices. I have found that in general the larger the customer, the worse the payment procedures. You do not want any delays in getting paid. In addition, experiment with some of these techniques:

Never start work without a signed purchase order or a deposit. For service businesses, try to secure a 25–50 percent deposit up front.

Negotiate and demand extended payment terms with vendors and suppliers. Try to get forty-five- to sixty-day payment terms.

Provide discounts to customers for early payment.

If you are on a long-term contract, try to negotiate payments a quarter ahead.

Factor invoices and purchase orders. Factoring involves selling an invoice to a company that will give you cash before your customer pays you for your goods or services. If you do this, you will give up 10–15 percent of the invoice, depending on the age of the receivable. Only use factoring when facing a significant cash shortfall.

Ask your corporate clients to pay your firm using Electronic Funds Transfer (EFT). Funds are wired directly to your business bank account with EFT, which means that your money is available five to ten days faster than a check sent by mail.

Make sure you can accept all forms of payment. Many firms now want to pay with a credit card.

EMERSON'S essentials

Never get mad at your money. *Do not ever be afraid to call a client about the status of payment. Don't be abusive or angry if a payment hasn't been made; instead, work with the client to ensure payment in a timely manner.*

Reduce initial labor costs by starting your staff on a "probationary wage" for three to six months. Delay the start of benefits until the end of the probation period.

Line of Credit

Managing cash flow is essential to the success of your small business. One way to accomplish this is to secure a line of credit. Structured much like your personal credit card, a line of credit allows you to tap into money as needed to stay on top of ongoing challenges.

A line of credit is suitable for temporary, short-term needs, such as purchasing supplies and inventory, and financing receivables. For larger, long-term investments, such as new facilities, equipment, and other fixed assets, a conventional business loan may be more appropriate.

Pay off the balance on your line of credit as soon as you can. Most credit lines are revolving, allowing you to reuse the funds as they are repaid. You do not want to build up a huge balance on a line of credit that you cannot pay.

You must make a significant number of payments on the principal of the loan each year. If you do not, the bank can classify you as an "abuser of your credit line." If this occurs, your line of credit will be termed out. Your credit is closed and transferred into a conventional term loan at a penalty interest rate.

If your bank sees that your business is in any financial jeopardy, they can send the loan to the workout unit in the bank. Once this happens, the bank will call the loan due immediately with a demand letter that will give the guarantors of the business line of credit ten business days to pay the loan in full. If your loan or line of credit lands in workout, the bank will move to liquidate your collateral or any assets you have. If you signed a personal guarantee for the loan, they are empowered to seize your personal assets.

The application and repayment requirements are generally far simpler for revolving lines of credit than for traditional loans. There are three kinds of revolving lines of credit:

1. One that is unsecured or only requires a personal guarantee,
2. One secured with collateral,
3. One that has an SBA guarantee.

Your application form will typically require two years of financial and operational information about your business, as well as your personal credit history.

A revolving line of credit is by no means the only cash-flow strategy for a small business. It is best to shop around for options and to line up your qualifications in advance, and to consider all the costs. Procedures to qualify for, to use, and to repay a revolving line of credit vary among banks. Nearly all banks charge start-up, transaction, and annual-use fees. Some also require annual reviews of how you're using your credit line, and, at will, your bank can transition your line of credit into a term loan with monthly automatic payments. A revolving line of credit offers the convenience of credit cards and many of the risks. Unlike loans, interest rates on a revolving line of credit may vary with the market, your payment history, and your balance owed. You must manage these funds wisely to make sure you do not abuse them.

Conventional Bank Loans

When it comes to finding a bank loan or a line of credit, the most important thing is you. Your own credit is your business credit. In the early period of your business, your personal credit history, more than anything else, will influence the bank's decision to lend you money. Banks are always reviewing lending practices and trying to minimize their risks. Particularly in periods of economic uncertainty, this scrutiny is even deeper for a loan to a small business.

Know your credit history before you go into a financial institution for a loan or line of credit. Make sure your credit information is accurate and up-to-date. If you can explain a late payment and know why it is on your credit file, offer your bank a reasonable explanation. It could make a big difference in getting an approval. The first step to getting the cash you need for your small business is to have a clean credit report.

There are other questions the bank or other financial institutions also will ask you:

Is your business sound? Have your business plan ready to show why your business is and will continue to be a success.

Why are you applying for this amount? Be specific about how much money you need, why you need it, and how you plan to use the funds.

How will you repay the loan? Outline your plan for repaying the money.

What guarantors can you offer as security? Specify what you are providing for collateral—banks like to know what they will need to do to recover a loan.

Getting bank loans can be challenging, but you can do it. Find out which banks in your market make the most small business loans. Ask other business owners about their banking relationships, and see if they will introduce you to their banker. In many cases, it is about whom you know and who knows you.

If you're looking for less than $100,000, many banks have a different program you can apply through. It will still require financial documentation, such as personal and business financial statements, tax returns for two years prior, and a personal credit score of the business owner(s). If you have a good personal credit score, it is somewhat easier to get approved and establish a line of credit for your business. If you manage your line properly for twelve to eighteen months, you will set the stage for requesting larger financing in the future.

Here is the list of items that many commercial banks will ask for during their evaluation process/underwriting process for financing greater than $100,000:

1. Personal financial statement (your net worth, excluding business value)
2. Personal tax return (past three years)
3. Business financial statements (past two years)
4. Business tax returns (federal, past two years)
5. Business financial statements—projections (one to two years), showing how the money will be spent and repaid
6. Business plan

If you have a media kit, press clips, or any customer testimonials, include this material with your loan application as well.

EMERSON'S essentials

Do not be afraid to apply for business credit, even if your business has not made a profit. *If you can show the bank how you anticipated and planned for a loss in the first three years, there should not be any issues.*

Apply to more than one financial institution. Not all banks evaluate loan packages the same way. Your list should include your present commercial bank, since you have already established a financial relationship there.

Look for institutions that may focus on a special category of business. For example, a bank may want to grant more loans in your neighborhood or to offer more loans to women-owned businesses, etc.

Work with a small business development center (SBDC) or a nonprofit that has a micro-lending program. Such groups often do loan packaging for deals under $50,000 and also have special business relationships with a number of financial institutions that will work hard to approve clients these groups send them. In addition, SBDCs may have other clients who have applied for credit and can guide you accordingly.

If you are denied credit, ask to speak with the underwriter and learn why your application did not score well. Take the time to address those areas and re-apply (usually a year later).

Many financial institutions will require a copy of your annual financial statements and tax returns, depending on the amount of your financing. They often relax this requirement after the first or second year and a minimum of twenty-four to thirty months of consistent on-time repayment.

As a business owner, you will always need money. Treat your banker as a valued relationship and you'll always have access to the money you need.

In a tight credit climate, it is essential to keep your personal credit score as high as possible. Banks will only make loans to business owners with pristine credit. Even the SBA will not be able to help your business if your personal credit score is below 650.

Keep in mind that *the SBA does not give business loans*. They provide guarantees to banks that provide business loans. You should find out from the local SBA office what are the top ten SBA lenders in your market so you'll know who's interested in loaning money to small businesses in your area. Depending on the type of loan the guarantee can be 50–75 percent of the loan amount. Having collateral and good credit greatly improves your chances of securing a business loan. Should the business become unable to pay its debt service, you will surrender the collateral.

The SBA is notorious for over-collateralizing loans. For example, the SBA's typical loan will require a lien on all current and future assets of the business. If you apply for a $25,000 SBA-guaranteed loan when you are a $100,000 business, after you become a bigger business and want to borrow more money, you will be prevented from using your additional assets to collateralize a new loan until your original loan is satisfied and the lien is removed.

EMERSON'S action steps

[1] Stay on top of your cash-flow management.

[2] Never start work without a signed purchase order or a deposit.

[3] Offer incentives to clients to pay early.

[4] Make sure you are set up to accept all forms of payment.

[5] Never be afraid to call a client about the status of payment.

[6] Develop a strong relationship with your bank so you can obtain a line of credit.

22

Maintaining Your Marketing

After your business has been launched, your marketing and advertising becomes more important than ever. The bounce that you get from the publicity accompanying your launch will soon dissipate unless you take active steps to keep the momentum going.

Advertising will be key to spreading your message beyond the initial circle of people you reached with your launch. As a small business owner with limited time and resources, you do not want to waste time guessing how to reach your customers. Test your advertising messages with focus groups and surveys before committing big dollars to a campaign. There are three criteria to consider when deciding how to reach your target customer with your marketing campaigns:

1. **Fit**. Your marketing must fit your brand image.
2. **Mix**. You must have the right selection of marketing methods to reach your target market.
3. **Cost**. Your marketing choices must fit your budget.

Traditional Advertising Options

Advertising includes newspapers/magazines, broadcast media, direct mailings, signage/billboards, promotional products, and tradeshows. Decide which of these advertising options is best for your business. Take note of which ones your competitor is using. Get a feel for how many leads each option will generate, and spend your dollars appropriately. It's best to start with how many leads a month you need to generate, and then determine the best method to make it happen.

Place ads in newspapers

Newspaper advertising works well for targeting mature demographics in local markets. Community papers are great for targeting specific neighborhoods. Start your campaign with small test ads and gradually expand as they prove effective. Feature the one or two sale items that you think will generate the most interest. Be sure to show a big percentage off the regular price.

Advantages
- Flexibility: advertising can vary from one locale to the next.
- A single Sunday newspaper can reach up to 60 percent of all homes and apartments.

Disadvantages
- Costs can also be an issue—shop carefully for the size ad that you need with the best chance for sales.
- Newspapers have a short lifespan, hasty reading, and relatively poor reproduction quality.
- Newspapers are struggling to stay in business.

Television commercials

Buying commercials on broadcast television is costly, but purchasing ad space through your local cable provider could be an affordable option. Keep in mind, television advertising is not a one-shot deal. It takes multiple television exposures before your message begins to penetrate the market. Regional cable could be a central element of a marketing strategy to establish you as a leader in the industry. It's best not to go this route, though, unless you have resources to maintain an effective campaign for at least three to six months.

Advantages
- Cable advertising is reasonably priced.
- You can target your audience by zip code.

Disadvantages
- There are production costs to create the commercial.
- Costs can quickly add up.
- While you can pick which cable channel your spots run on, you do not always get to pick when they run.

Signage

There are many ways to use signage in your small business. In addition to making sure the customers know what door to knock on, bright colorful signage with the business phone number clearly displayed outside of the building attracts walk-in traffic. A few strategically placed billboards on well-traveled streets in your local community could be a great investment for your new small business.

Advantages
- Well-done signage is a cost-effective marketing tool that will keep customers coming to your door.
- Building and auto signage is typically a one-time expense.

Disadvantages

- Poorly done signage that is hard to read is worse than no signage at all.
- Billboard signage can be pricey over time. If you go with a community billboard strategy, make sure you have a budget to keep your signage up for at least six months.

Publish ads in free tabloids

Many of these (often called "shoppers") are distributed locally through mailings, on public transportation, in shopping malls, or in other outlets.

Advantages

- Such ads are low cost.
- They have very targeted geographic distribution.

Disadvantages

- The size and number of ads in free tabloids could make it difficult for your products/services to stand out.
- Free newspapers are often discarded because they are considered "junk."

Consider using direct mail

You can rent a consumer or business mailing list to contact potential customers. You can even request lists with specific demographic information. Generally, the more detail you need on the mailing label, the higher the cost, which can range from $50–$250 per thousand names. When designing your mailing, keep these things in mind: You need to get to the point quickly. Anticipate consumer questions and answer them in your sales copy. Be informative. Do not try to intimidate the reader. Use a professional graphic designer to lay out the mailer.

Advantages
- You can select a list by zip code or a narrow geographic area.
- You can also get lists for a specific target group—homeowners, senior citizens, particular types of businesses, etc.
- You can adjust the list for future mailings.

Disadvantages
- Much of direct mail is automatically considered junk mail.
- The task of grabbing a consumer's attention is no small order.
- It can be very expensive because you pay for design, printing, and postage, and you can only use the list for a limited number of mailings.

Radio advertising

Radio commercials can be recorded and broadcast quickly and relatively inexpensively. Most standard AM/FM radio stations are great for local advertising. Be aware that timing is everything in the radio advertising industry. Morning and evening drive times are the most expensive times to advertise.

Advantages
- Production cost is low. Usually the station will produce the spot with one of their on-air personalities.
- Drivers are a captive audience.
- You can advertise to a specific target market.
- Radio can help build a larger client base.

Disadvantages
- Radio is temporary and requires a lot of repetition, which can be costly.
- To reach a wider market, you may need to run advertising on multiple radio stations.

Promotional items

When you have a grand opening, give out promotional items to keep your business in your customers' thoughts. You can put your company's name and logo on anything; calendars, flash drives, t-shirts, pens/pencils, notepads, sticky pads, mugs, etc.

Advantages

- Customers like free stuff, especially if it is useful.
- It's an ongoing reminder of your company's product or service.
- Putting your company's brand out in the marketplace can encourage repeat business and helps differentiate you from your competitors.

Disadvantages

- Promotional trinkets cost money and are no guarantee of success.
- Generally, space on such items is very limited for your message and contact information.

EMERSON'S action steps

[1] Plan your postlaunch marketing around the idea of firming your initial customer base and expanding it.

[2] Stick to your marketing budget.

[3] Pick the advertising methods best suited to engage your prospective customers.

[4] Focus on ideas that generate repeat business.

23

TEN THINGS YOU MUST NEVER FORGET IN BUSINESS

This chapter is what I call common sense information about business, information that is easy to forget over time. It's not just enough to quit your job and start your own business. These are the ten things that will keep you in business if you put them into practice.

If you take this chapter seriously and practice what I preach here, you will shave three years off of your learning curve as a new business owner. Trust me! This chapter focuses on understanding your profit model, friendliness, the art of the close, paying attention, presentation is everything, time is money, the importance of confirming the deal, encouraging feedback, managing the customer experience, and the importance of always be looking for the next customer.

1. Make Sure You Know How Much Profit Is in Every Deal

This may seem like common sense, but it is not! Before you send pricing to any client, it is important to figure out what the job is worth to you. Early on in my business, I had a one-size-fits-all pricing model. When I started analyzing my profits, I was lucky if I made 25 percent gross revenue on any project. I still had to pay all overhead and taxes from that before I pocketed any money. This system got me nowhere fast.

What are some of the things you need to consider in determining your profit? Let's say you run a tailoring business, for example. Here are some things to consider:

Cost of materials—If you make suits or dresses, track the expense of fabric, buttons, thread, and trim for each garment you make.

Cost of labor—If you are doing the work yourself, what is your time worth? $10/hour? $20/hour? $75/hour or more? Are you designing the garment yourself or is the customer giving you the specifications? If you are paying an employee or freelancer to do the work, how much time will it take for him or her to make the garment? *Your time is your money.*

Overhead—Businesses use many things that are not free—electricity, heat, rent, insurance, water, business licenses, advertising, legal fees, security, accounting costs, computers, software, cash registers, and other office supplies. Some things are occasional expenses; others are weekly or monthly. All of them are things that must be paid for by your business and should be reflected in your price. You should know how much money it costs you to run your business monthly, which is also known as your monthly burn rate.

How much margin is enough?

Once you have calculated your costs, decide what you are going to charge the customer. If you see yourself as a premier tailor whose craftsmanship is recognized as clearly superior by your customers (and remember, the important thing is that *your customers have to see you that way*), you may able to get away with very high profit margins. Gucci, Valentino, and some high-end tailors like Jon Green get $6,000 to $7,000 per suit, based on the perception of status that the name implies. On the other end, you can get a Hong Kong suit delivered in the United States for $500–$1,000, depending on fabric. The lower labor cost increases the per-unit margin of each suit, but you will need to sell more of them to match the revenue of the high-end option. My suggestion is that you start your pricing at 100 percent to 150 percent above cost, depending on the market, your competition, and your customer base.

EMERSON'S essentials

If you don't have a background in accounting, make sure you get sound advice on your finances. *You can learn some really expensive lessons if you do not understand profit margins upfront.*

You can always reduce prices, run sales, and create promotional events to get customers in the door. But remember, you must cover your costs, or you will end up broke and out of business.

Steve McKee, author of *When Growth Stalls*, says that if you are going to discount your products, do it briefly, credibly, and creatively. Discounting briefly is just that, offering a discount for a short time. Discounting credibly means not compromising your brand for a sale. Discounting creatively means planning each of your discounts and making them part of your overall business plan. Don't just slap a 25-percent-off sticker on the whole store. Rather, explain that you are introducing a more economical line of services to expand the client base.

EMERSON'S experience

Once I figured out that I wasn't making enough money on my projects, I sat down with my accountant and created a spreadsheet that told me exactly how much each job was costing me. My accountant also formatted my accounting software to track project expenses. I began to see how much profit there was in a given project.

The costing breakdown forced me to justify my pricing, rather than determining pricing by using "gut" feelings or what I thought the customer would pay.

2. Customer Service Is the Truth, the Light, and the Way

There are times in business when you will make a mistake. It happens to everyone; the key is how you fix it. Once a furious client called me the day after the Christmas holiday wanting to know where her company's product was. She said, "We've paid you all your money, so where is our merchandise?"

I was stunned because I had directed a subcontractor to deliver the products weeks earlier. I apologized for the mistake and assured her I would get on it right away.

I tracked down what had happened (the subcontractor hadn't done his job) and fixed the problem. I also sent my client a fruit basket to apologize again for the mistake, and to re-affirm our relationship. The upshot was that I was able to keep the customer and eliminate a subcontractor who was hurting my reputation.

This is just a small example of what every small business owner has to deal with every day. Here are some rules for giving great customer service:

Always know the value of a customer

Know how much profit your customer puts in your pocket. Have a strategy for turning a new customer into a long-term customer. Go the extra yard to make your customers happy, and treat them like your paycheck—because they are.

Generate positive "buzz" and great word-of-mouth

Excellent customer satisfaction is the best advertising you can get in business. We all try new businesses based on a friend's recommendation. Work hard to get folks to say great things about *your* business. Unhappy customers will tell the world about your poor product or bad service.

Stay positive

Customers get mad, but you can't afford an angry response. Most people really just want to vent. Always be professional, be willing to listen, and prepared to meet the customer more than halfway to solve a dispute. Only in the most extreme of circumstances should you say, "Absolutely not." Say it too often, and you'll be out of business.

Look for feedback

Ask for customer feedback. Use surveys, and always call your customers after you provide service to see what you can do you to increase their satisfaction (and your sales). Use customer intelligence to learn about industry trends and increase your product offerings. The more you know about serving your customer, the more competitive your business will be.

3. ABC—"Always Be Closing"

This is an easy way to remember that new business can come to you at any time and just about from any place. Here are some key rules:

Religious persistence

Call, knock on doors, and e-mail your contacts. Be relentless in going after your target customers. A percentage of those folks getting your messages will eventually contact you, and when the time is right, you *will* get the business.

Create targeted marketing materials

No matter what business you are in, you need to gear your marketing and promotional materials to a specific audience. If you own a car wash, distributing flyers in the neighborhoods close by may be the way to go.

Close, close, close!

You must ask for the business! If you see potential customers, ask for an appointment. Ask if they are happy with their current supplier. Even if they are ecstatic with their current supplier, invite them to lunch; offer a limited time discount. Ask them what it will take to get their business.

4. Pay Attention to Detail

Customers are risk-averse. It is hard to gain a customer's confidence until you can show them that you can fix their problems without creating more. They may already have a long-term relationship with another business, and you are the unproven new kid on the block. Here are some priorities for making the best first impression.

Well-written marketing and/or collateral materials

Make your message to a potential customer direct and to the point. The benefits and features of doing business with your company should be clear. Be sure to spell out your unique value proposition. Please have someone else read your drafts before you get anything printed. I can't stress this enough. There's nothing worse than spending your limited resources on printing 1,000 copies of something with a typo glaring out at the reader.

Effective meeting management

Make sure when you are meeting with clients that your comments are thoughtful and brief. Do more listening than talking. Respect your client's time. If she says she has only twenty minutes, that is all the time *you* have. If you keep her forty-five minutes, you have guaranteed you will not be asked back. Finally, make sure to focus on what you want the outcome of this meeting to be, whether it is a next step or finalizing a contract.

EMERSON'S essentials

Sometimes computers and projectors do not work properly, so have copies of your presentation ready to hand out. *In fact, always make three more copies than you think you'll need. Clients like to invite extra people to group meetings.*

Responding to a bid request

Make sure your proposal is organized with tabs in a binder or presentation folder. Present a proposal so polished that, in effect, you dare the audience not to award your company the contract, even if your bid isn't the lowest. The first page of every proposal I send says, "Why your business needs Melinda Emerson." I customize my bid covers to the particular service needed in the RFP so they know why my consulting services are the solution to many of their small business marketing problems.

5. Nothing Beats a Professional Presentation

Don't try to bring your "A game" in your "B suit." How you look and how you speak sends a message to the customer. Bad impressions are often deal breakers because they go directly to trust. People are reluctant to spend money on vendors who don't look right for the services or products that they are representing.

EMERSON'S experience

I once knew a woman who would bring a fresh suit to her office every time she had any sales appointments. She would actually change suits in the middle of the day if she had morning and afternoon appointments. She told me, "As a woman who wears makeup, if makeup is on your collar or clothes, it absolutely looks unprofessional, and you need to change."

At the time I thought she was vain, but later, as my business matured, I started to notice how the most effective salespeople looked when they showed up to sales calls and trade shows, and I realized that she was right. Now, I'm not saying you should go out and buy a whole new wardrobe, but we all know which are our best suits. Use the best when you are selling for your business.

Speaking the part

It is said that no one knows who you are until you open your mouth. That not only applies to having good dental work. When they hear you speak, people make judgments about your education, class, intelligence, and most importantly, about whether you can do the job or deliver the service. It is an unfair and biased approach to evaluating a potential vendor, but life is not fair. First impressions can leave lasting damage or be the first step to a big contract. Practice, practice, practice getting your message out in a clear, concise, and professional way. Open that customer's "comfort zone" so that he will let you and your message in the door.

6. Time Is the Most Valuable Asset in Your Business

As an entrepreneur, your time is the most valuable thing that you can give anyone, so treat it as such. Qualify that your prospective client is ready to do business before you agree to meet with them. If the client does not yet have a budget, perhaps they are not ready to buy. Conduct as much prework over the phone as possible, and develop a checklist of things you need from the client prior to developing a quote or attending a meeting. If you can, make the meeting in your office, so that you lose less time if he doesn't show up.

EMERSON'S essentials

Confirm appointments a day in advance. *When I schedule an appointment, I always get the cell number of the person with whom I am meeting. If I'm lost or might possibly be late, I can make a courtesy call.*

Here are some hints to manage your time more effectively:

Be early for appointments
You can waste your time, but not your client's. That's the cost of being an entrepreneur. Check for traffic jams, have an idea of what

parking is available near your client, check the weather, and allow time for the walk to the building. There is no time for surprises when you are trying to get to an appointment.

EMERSON'S experience

Early on in my business, I began to get a reputation for being late. Then one of my mentors said someone had mentioned my problem to her. I realized my reputation was spreading and could damage my business. From then on, I have been the first one to arrive at any meeting I attend. The key to being a good business owner is to take good advice and respond immediately. Like it or not, most of your customers run on the clock and have a bias against people who waste their time by not keeping appointments promptly.

Make a "to do" and a "call list" list with priorities

There is a lot to do when you are in business—and a lot of it's nonbusiness stuff, from paying bills, setting aside time for social events, or meeting with your child's teachers. Make your list, ranking the "must do's" and the "should do's," so you can easily see how much time you have to work with that day.

Never say "yes" when you need to say "no"

Nonessential activities like nonprofit boards or volunteer projects can be quicksand for your time, sucking you up until you can barely breathe. Unless there is a real, quantifiable business benefit or a key personal reason for an activity to be on your list of priorities, just say *no*.

EMERSON'S essentials

When you are in business, everyone thinks you have lots of money. *That is the goal, but not always the reality. Be strategic about what fundraisers and social events you attend. Check the organization's board list to see if any "big fish" you need to meet could be in attendance.*

7. Get It in Writing

My brother is an attorney, and he has a saying: "A conversation never happened until you get it in writing." There will be times in your business when you deal with clients who promise you things or tell you it's a deal, and then things fall apart. Do yourself a favor: Do not start any work or ship any product until you get a signed contract or purchase order.

Clients are sometimes subject to the internal politics of their companies. For example, someone gives you a green light for a project when they really needed approval from someone else. There's no such thing as a handshake deal or verbal agreement. Get everything in writing.

Send follow-up memos and e-mails

Make sure everyone is clear as to expectations and deliverables, especially when your clients need to provide information. Make sure you know the names and titles of the people you are working with and where they fit in the corporate structure. Always ask for business cards.

EMERSON'S experience

I was doing a project by committee, and my client needed to provide me with a lot of materials to prepare the project. However, the contact person who was supposed to gather the material didn't like me, and was not concerned about when I got the materials.

I got in touch with a friend inside my client's organization who suggested I reiterate my contact's task list in writing, using a friendly, nonthreatening tone. I did so and sent copies to a few key people in the client organization.

In doing this, I took a risk, since you can make enemies of people if you expose them to their superiors. At the same time, I did three things for myself.

1. I put into writing what I was expecting.
2. I covered myself in case we did not make deadline for the project.
3. I got an immediate response.

Always send a client a memo after a meeting to clarify what was discussed and agreed to as far as action steps.

8. Use Reference Letters as Report Cards

Ask for a reference letter from clients. There are several reasons to do this: it helps to build your business, provides constructive feedback, and encourages the client to think about their experience with your company. If a client won't give a letter, you need to know why. You need to make sure you are doing an excellent job. The letter will help you understand what you could have done better, and what the customer liked about doing business with your company. People like to see letters as proof of your good track record. You can use the testimonials in your collateral materials.

9. Manage Your Client's First Impression

There is nothing worse than calling a place of business and having someone unprofessional or rude answer the phone. The person answering the phone is your first line of offense, someone who indicates the culture of your business and your brand. You must make sure this person is polite, friendly, and helpful.

Here are some hints to make that telephone call as impressive as a face-to-face meeting:

Answer promptly—The phone should be answered in no more than two to three rings.

Identify the company, then yourself—"Good morning, This is Melinda Emerson's office. Sonia speaking. How may I help you?" When your clients call you, they should encounter someone just like you. The receptionist should be someone who is helpful and professional with solid verbal skills, who speaks clearly, slowly, and in a pleasant voice.

"May I put you on hold"—Teach your receptionist to ask before putting a caller on hold and to apologize for doing so when she returns back on line. If the party the caller is looking for is not there, make sure your receptionist can connect the caller to the party's voicemail or offers to take a message.

For home-based businesses

Get separate phone and fax lines for your business and use voice-mail. I would also suggest using an answering service and forwarding the phone to your cell phone to increase responsiveness. Do not broadcast how small your business is by using the family answering machine.

10. Always Fill the Pipeline

No matter what else is going on, always know from where your next bit of business is going to come. In the fourth quarter, I'm already working on contracts for the first quarter of the next calendar year.

Here are some strategies you might find useful:

Get information on your client's budget schedule

You must constantly be working your contacts to find out when they are planning budgets and when their budgets close. With that information, you can position your projects and activities for that client so that money for those projects will be earmarked in their budget.

Nurture your relationships

Turn contacts into contracts by staying in touch. Don't just buy contact management software—use it. Call every quarter to check in, send an e-blast, and mail holiday cards. Make sure you thank all your customers for their business. If your customer has awarded your firm a significant large contract that year, send a gift for the holidays.

EMERSON'S essentials

Make sure that sending a thank-you or holiday gift is not against your client's company policy. *I have a contact at Wal-Mart who is not even allowed to accept lunch, let alone a holiday gift. All you want is to keep your name on the list of contacts that people call when they have a need; hopefully your name is at the top of the list.*

Prospect everywhere and all the time

Make sure everyone in your circle knows what you do and has enough information about your company to refer people to it. Read your local business journals, business magazines, and daily newspaper's business section to find RFP advertisements and leads. Attend seminars, business opportunity breakfasts, and procurement events to constantly meet people who might be new contacts who could generate some business. The small business development centers, chambers of commerce, minority and women's business organizations sponsor these kinds of events monthly. Take full advantage of every opportunity to fill your pipeline.

24

FINAL THOUGHTS

Today you should start thinking of your job as a temporary situation. You will do what you have to do so you can do what you want to do. You now have a roadmap for long-term business success. Plan your life, then plan your business.

You now know what it takes to develop a life plan, financially reposition yourself, solidify your business idea, develop the marketing strategy, and then write the business plan. Key to all of your entrepreneurial dreams coming true will be your ability to manage your finances and save. Start cutting back your expenses today. Use a budget and engage your whole family in its development. Make sure you spouse or family is behind you. Plan for all the insurance you will need (health, life, disability).

EMERSON'S essentials

Everybody's got good ideas and skills, but that doesn't mean they should become an entrepreneur. *The business of running a business is an entirely different matter.*

Be very discreet about your business plans. Use the five-finger rule: Don't tell more than five people about your idea, including your momma. Be honest with yourself about what skills you have and what skills you will need to run your business. Think about who you are going to need to help you to be successful in your business venture. Invest in a PDA cell phone so you can always stay connected.

Find a small business development center in your area and make an appointment. Start thinking about your marketing strategy and your business plan. Remember, your business plan is a living, breathing document that should be reviewed and updated every one to two months in the first year of business to make sure your business is on the right track.

Work Your Network

Are you known more internally or externally at your job? You need to become a networking machine. Make new friends and use this planning year to reconnect with old contacts. People do business with people they like and know. Hone your selling skills by joining small business organizations and networking groups. Practice putting yourself out there.

The key to effective networking is building a genuine relationship first, then promoting your product or service. The rules are the same whether you are selling life insurance, designer shirts, or a home security system installation. The bedrock of entrepreneurship is word-of-mouth referrals. If people not only like you but also believe in what you are selling, you have a valuable marketing tool that will keep on generating business for you.

Remember the 7 Essential Principles of Small Business Success

1. Have an entrepreneurial mindset.
2. Observe strict fiscal discipline.
3. Form a kitchen cabinet of advisors to support you.
4. Have a defined brand.
5. Focus on a niche market.
6. Provide excellent customer service.
7. Understand your cash position and carefully manage your banking relationship.

Brand Your Business

Think about and work on your brand image. Hire a professional graphic designer to create your logo. Make sure your customers can find you online.

In this cyber age, developing an online marketing strategy must be a priority. It all starts with a niche-targeted website. Then use your social media activities to drive traffic to your website. Upgrade your technology skills. Don't be afraid to hire someone to help you get up to speed on the latest social media networking sites quickly. Learn the culture of these sites first, so that you can plan how you will use them to boost your networking. Learn web-authoring software.

Claim Success from the Beginning

If you do not believe in your success, no one else will. Before you do anything in your business, tell people about the great results you're expecting to achieve. Some people may be naysayers in the beginning, but stay focused on the end result. You may have potential clients who will waste your time or refuse to give you a meeting. Find a quote, phrase, or Bible verse that inspires you. Print it out and tape it to the wall. On hard days, read it out loud.

Grow Yourself

Make yourself a student of small business. That's what I did. My nickname is SmallBizLady. My slogan is Grow Yourself to Grow Your Business. You need to learn all you can about the business of running a business in order to be successful. There is a whole business world out there that you do not know much about yet.

You are going to have some tough days ahead. Business ownership is not easy. If it were, one out of three business owners would not fail in their second year of operation. My father used to say, "You wouldn't know good days if it weren't for bad days." Savor all your good days in your business.

Get yourself a theme song

Pick a song that always makes you feel good and gives you energy. Keep a copy everywhere (car, office, iPod). In the middle of the day, hit YouTube.com to listen for some emergency inspiration. Play your song every day to help remind you of your small business goal.

Make the difference clear

Take time to develop your signature move. What will be your competitive advantage? Figure out what really makes your business unique and different. What is your niche? How will you compete? On service? On price? As a one-stop option? With limited time and resources, the more narrow your focus, the easier it will be to plan your marketing efforts. Remember, it is your mindset that can hold you back.

Set SMART goals

A goal is nothing more than a dream with a deadline. Remember to set **S**pecific, **M**easurable, **A**ttainable, **R**ealistic, and **T**imely goals. Nothing is a bigger turn-off to a potential investor than unrealistic financial projections. Make a timeline for your process, and give yourself milestones to hit. Think, I am going to be debt-free in six months.

Key to realizing your dreams is to organize your time. Give your business venture two hours a day for starters. Stop watching television, and go to bed earlier so you're well rested.

Save for Retirement!

Once you start generating an income from your business, save for retirement! Consider placing a percentage of your income every year in a SEP-IRA or other small business retirement account. SEP accounts are easy to set up, and your contributions are tax deductible. Once your account is established, you can contribute every year up to your tax filing deadline, including any extensions. Your contributions can vary each year, offering you some flexibility when business or personal conditions vary.

I wrote this book because I love entrepreneurs. You are the bravest people on the planet. You create jobs, provide benefits to people, and provide the highest quality of service to your customers. Being a small business owner is a spiritual journey; you will be stretched in ways that you cannot imagine. The best thing you can do for your business is to pray every day, and remember that you and God do not wear the same watch. His timing is perfect. And if you even find your business in a rut, re-read this book. Here are my four bits of advice for small business success:

> Live your life plan!
> Love something other than your business!
> Laugh at yourself!
> Learn every day!

If I have helped you, please e-mail me at *Melinda@melindaemerson.com* and tell me your story. I love to hear from dedicated entrepreneurs. Be flexible. Stay positive and encouraged. Good luck.

APPENDIX A

SAMPLE CUSTOMER SATISFACTION SURVEY

Here's a sample customer service survey you can use to understand your customer's experience with your business.

We thank you for your business. Please provide us with your feedback on a scale from 1 to 5, using this criteria:

1 = Poor 2 = Fair 3 = Good 4 = Very Good 5 = Excellent

Did you have a good shopping experience? _____

Was the staff courteous and helpful? _____

Did you find everything you needed? _____

Did you receive good value for the price? _____

What could have improved your buying experience? _____

Would you do business with us again? _____

Would you refer us to a friend or colleague? _____

Do you have any additional feedback? _____

_____

_____

_____

May we contact you for additional comment?

❑ Yes
❑ No

Name _____

Phone /e-mail _____

Appendix B

Further Resources

Book References

Ten books that you should have in your small business library:

1. *How to Win Friends and Influence People* by Dale Carnegie
2. *The 25 Most Common Sales Mistakes and How to Avoid Them* by Stephan Schiffman
3. *Guerilla Marketing for Small Businesses* by Jay Conrad Levinson
4. *Finance for Non-Finance Managers and Small Business Owners* by Lawrence W. Tuller
5. *Entrepreneurial Finance: Finance and Business Strategies for the Serious Entrepreneur* by Steven Rogers
6. *This Is How We Do It: A Practical Guide for the Working Mother* by Carol Evans
7. *The Ultimate Guide to Electronic Marketing for Small Businesses* by Tom Antion

8. *The Seven Minute Difference* by Allyson Lewis
9. *The New Rules of Marketing & PR* by David Meerman Scott
10. *Small Giants* by Bo Burlingham

If you buy business books and never get around to reading them, consider subscribing to Soundview Executive Book Summaries, *www.summary.com*. This company provides concise summaries of recently published business books.

Federal Resources

Census Bureau
The Census Bureau serves as the leading source of quality data about the nation's people and economy.
www.census.gov

U.S. Copyright Office
101 Independence Avenue SE
Washington, DC 20559-6000
(202) 707-3000
www.copyright.gov

Department of Labor
The Department of Labor promotes the welfare of the job seekers, wage earners, and retirees of the United States. They also track changes in employment, prices, and other national economic measurements.
www.dol.gov

Export.gov
A federal resource for information about markets and industries throughout the world.
www.export.gov

Federal Business Opportunity
The federal government's one-stop virtual marketplace for all federal contracts.
www.Fedbizopps.gov

Internal Revenue Service
The IRS has a Small Business and Self-Employed Tax Center
www.irs.gov/businesses/small

Minority Business Development Agency (MBDA)
This agency, part of the U.S. Department of Commerce, was created to foster the establishment and growth of minority-owned businesses in America.
Call for locations: 1-888-324-1551
www.mbda.gov

National Ombudsman (SBA program)
The National Ombudsman's primary mission is to assist small businesses when they experience excessive or unfair federal regulatory enforcement actions.
www.sba.gov/aboutsba/sbaprograms/ombudsman/index.html

Occupational Safety and Health Administration (OSHA)
The Federal Occupational Safety and Health Administration (OSHA) outlines specific health and safety standards employers must provide for the protection of employees.
www.osha.gov/dcsp/smallbusiness/index.html

Small Business Administration (SBA)

The Small Business Administration provides information and resources that will help you at any stage of the business lifecycle.

www.sba.gov/smallbusinessplanner/index.html

SBDCNet

The Small Business Development Center National Information Clearinghouse serves as a resource providing timely, relevant research, web-based information, and training to SBDC counselors and their small business clients.

www.sbdcnet.org

Service Corps of Retired Executives

SCORE is the best source of free and confidential small business advice to help you build your business.

www.score.org

Trademark Assistance Center

1-800-786-9199, or e-mail *TrademarkAssistanceCenter@uspto .gov*

www.uspto.gov

Womenbiz.gov

This site is the gateway for women-owned businesses selling to the federal government.

www.womenbiz.gov

For a more extensive list of web-based resources available to the aspiring small business owner, visit my website at *www .smallbizlady.com.*

Web Resources

AllBusiness.com

This site has tons of small business information and sample forms and agreements. They have expert podcasts and videos on business topics as well.

www.allbusiness.com

Alltop.com

Under the heading "small business," Alltop has links to more than 100 different sites, including small-business related news and stories, and opinions and blogs.

www.alltop.com

Austin Family Business Program

Information and advice for running and working in a family business.

www.familybusinessonline.org

Bizstats.com

Instant access to useful financial ratios, business statistics, and benchmarks.

www.bizstats.com

Bplans.com

The largest single collection of free sample business plans online. The site also includes interactive tools and a panel of experts.

www.bplans.com

Business Owner's Tool Kit
More than 5,000 pages of free cost-cutting tips, step-by-step checklists, real-life case studies, start-up advice, and business templates for small business owners and entrepreneurs.
www.toolkit.com

Center for Women's Business Research
This is the go-to source on the trends, characteristics, achievements, and challenges concerning women business owners and their enterprises.
www.nfwbo.org

Dun & Bradstreet
The world's leading source of commercial information and insight on businesses. You should obtain a DUNS number to establish business credibility.
www.dnb.com

Entrepreneurship.org
This site for high-growth business development was developed and funded by the Kauffman Foundation, the world's largest foundation dedicated to entrepreneurship.
www.entrepreneurship.org

Family Business Institute
Consulting with family business ventures since 1995
www.familybusinessinstitute.com/additional-resources/13.html

Fedmarket.com
More than 100 pages of valuable procurement-related articles, information, and links about marketing your services to the government. The site also offers live seminars and trade shows.
www.fedmarket.com

Franchise Registry

Helps lenders speed access to SBA financial assistance during the loan review process for franchisees. The Registry enables lenders and SBA local offices to verify a franchise system's lending eligibility through the Internet.

www.franchiseregistry.com

FranNet

Franchise experts help you learn about the many choices available and how to select the right opportunity for you.

www.frannet.com

Hoover's, Inc.

The service delivers comprehensive company, industry, and market intelligence on more than 14 million companies, with in-depth coverage of 42,000 of the world's top businesses. Reports are generated for a fee.

www.hoovers.com

IBISWorld

IBISWorld is a leader in gathering business data to help you do industry analysis. This is a fee-based service.

www.ibisworld.com

Microsoft Small Business Center

Provides advice, products, technology tools and information for small businesses.

www.microsoft.com/smallbusiness/hub.mspx

MoreBusiness.com

A wealth of useful articles, sample business plans, business tips, insight, a free Intranet, and other material to help small businesses grow.

www.morebusiness.com

NOLO

The nation's leading provider of do-it-yourself legal solutions for small businesses. Their goal is to help people handle their own everyday legal matters or learn enough about them to make working with a lawyer a more satisfying experience.

www.nolo.com/category/sb_home.html

Public Entity Risk Institute (PERI)

High-quality risk management information, training, data, and data analysis. The website also features an extensive resource library organized by topic, audience, and type of resource.

www.riskinstitute.org/peri

Zoomerang

Online software that businesses, organizations, and individuals can use to create professional, customized surveys.

www.zoomerang.com

Index